THE
KAIROS
Adventure

NEIGHBORING IN GOD'S TIMING

LYNN CORY

"I have no greater joy than to hear that my children are walking in the truth" (3 John 1:4).

Dedicated to my three sons, David, Paul, and Adam. I have no greater joy than to know that each of you is walking in the truth. *The Kairos Adventure* is my legacy which I leave to the three of you. May the Lord give you the grace and wisdom to invest it well in God's kingdom, and may the Lord's church benefit greatly from your investment.
I love each of you deeply!

ISBN-13: 978-0-9978601-2-2

Cover design by Nadine Erickson

Printed in the United States of America

Contents

Foreword

Our lives with God are frequently compared to a journey. It all began with Abraham in Genesis 12:4: "So Abram went, as the LORD had told him." He heard the call, took a huge risk, and began a lifelong journey with God. I don't know if your experience is like mine, but my life has been a series of journeys. Every time I arrive at a new destination and get settled, the Lord calls me to another journey.

My very first adventure with Jesus began almost fifty years ago when He called me to travel through the Bible. It was all very new to me, but what an exciting trip as I studied from Genesis to Revelation. His Word forever changed my life.

Later in life, God called me to missions. I've had the privilege of journeying with Jesus to more than a dozen nations to teach, preach, bring medical relief, care for the needy, and encourage local churches. The call to missions comes right from the heart of God, and short-term mission trips have thrilled millions of believers. As a result, many have answered the call to relocate to foreign lands just like the early apostles.

Recently, many Christians have been called to "the journey inward," as Peter Scazzerro, the most popular author on the subject, wrote in *Emotionally Healthy Spirituality*. Although Pete was a successful pastor accomplishing great things for God, he discovered that he was neither emotionally nor spiritually healthy. He saw his life as an iceberg. The 10 percent people could see looked great, but what lay below the surface was in shambles. God's Spirit began to help him with both his interior life and his devotional life. As he went deeper with God, he discovered a new richness. The journey of spiritual formation is much needed in the Church today.

There are numerous other journeys many of us have been called to embark upon. Perhaps you have traveled through the grief process, a career change, marriage and family challenges, or addiction recovery. Maybe you've entered into the so-called "Golden Years." Life involves many such shifts, but the good news is that Jesus is always faithful to travel with us.

A number of years ago, Lynn Cory invited me to embark on a new journey. We had worked together in full-time ministry for almost thirty years. Lynn is an exceptional man and pastor. I don't know how our church would have survived without his wisdom, character, faithfulness, and commitment to God's kingdom. Yet, Lynn came up with a crazy idea about a radical direction he believed Jesus was calling us to take. It wasn't surprising.

Lynn had come up with radical ideas before. Years ago, God called him to build a Jewish-Christian fellowship and take teams to Israel. This wasn't a Holy Land tour, but a ministry trip to serve among Jews and Palestinians while tensions were high. Then there was the season when he called us to journey with him in performing random acts of kindness in our community. We found ourselves partnering with the LAPD and other civic leaders. We sent teams throughout our valley to bless people by cleaning up neglected areas, trimming trees, hanging Christmas lights, and doing similar projects. Every outing was an adventure and supported by intensive prayer. Many people took the risk and joined us on this journey.

But then Lynn went a bit too far. We wondered if he was mentally sound because he came up with an extreme idea. He was bold enough to suggest that God was calling us to take a new and frightening journey to reach (brace yourself) our next-door neighbors. To those of us living in Los Angeles, this seemed bizarre. Here in L.A. we ignore our neighbors; they ignore us. It's a very comfortable arrangement and works well. We are polite about it. We even wave once in a while.

We wondered if Lynn had come up with some sort of new doctrine. But actually, he discovered an obscure passage in the Bible that contains this command: "Love your neighbor." (This "obscure" command is repeated three times in the Old Testament and a whopping fifteen times in the New Testament.) Lynn really thought he had us cornered, but we were prepared. We responded, "Who is my neighbor?" (See Luke 10:29.) Maybe my neighbor is the person I sit next to in church? Maybe my neighbor is one of my Facebook friends? "I'm loving them!"

We are a tough crowd, so Lynn broke down the Greek and the Hebrew word used in the relevant scriptures and then informed us that the English word for neighbor comes from "nigh," as in close, and "boer." A boer is a farmer. In other words, the people who live next door. We were shocked. Many of us had traveled to the mountains of Mexico and war-torn regions of Israel. Would Lynn go so far as to expect us to journey… across the street?

Yes, I'm having a bit of fun with this, but it's ironic that Lynn has had to write several books and travel to church after church to convince Christians that God wants us to reach our neighbors. As Lynn has invited us into this journey, thousands of people have taken that step and seen the Lord do great things right where they live. That is what this book is about. It's filled with stories of people who have stepped out to love their neighbors and have found it to be an exciting journey. I'm certain you will enjoy these stories, but our hope is that you will take your first steps to join us on this journey and see what the Lord will do.

—*Bill Dwyer*

Bill is the founding pastor of Valley Vineyard Christian Fellowship in Reseda, California, and a team member with both Dallas Willard Ministries and Foundation for His Ministry. He has been a great supporter of Neighborhood Initiative over the years and has made it a practice to love and care for his own neighbors.

Acknowledgments

I thank God for His enduring love for me and for encouraging me to write *The Kairos Adventure*. I never dreamed that I would write a book, let alone three books. By God's grace this book has come to be, because He desires that we in the Church love our neighbors as ourselves.

I thank God for dear jo, my wife, for her support as I have written yet another book. I am grateful for all her input as I worked on the manuscript.

I am deeply grateful to those who contributed to *The Kairos Adventure*; this is our book. Your compelling stories have influenced my life, and I trust they will inspire others in the Lord's Church to love their neighbors and spread this kind of love beyond the neighborhoods where God has placed them.

I thank my three dear friends, Anthony Rodriguez, John Tolle, and Bahram Khayatpour, whom I meet with each week so we can encourage one another and pray that the Lord will move the love of neighbors forward in and through His Church. Your personal support has been invaluable to me.

I am indebted to the Neighborhood Initiative prayer team and the Tuesday Morning Prayer Group for praying for Neighborhood Initiative (NI) and *The Kairos Adventure*, and for all your support.

I am grateful to all of those in the Lord's Church who have stepped up to make their homes lighthouses, so to speak, so that the love of Jesus will touch their actual neighbors.

I thank God for my dear neighbors—Andra Berkolds, Mike and Donna Handy, Liane Reynolds, Dana Langdon, and Gary Schneider—whom my wife and I meet with every week to study the Scriptures, laugh, eat, pray, and intentionally love our neighbors. Each of you have been a great encouragement to jo and me.

I thank God for Bill Dwyer, my pastor, who has encouraged me with NI since its inception. You will read about how NI came to be, from his perspective, in this book's foreword. Some years back, he walked into my office and strongly suggested that I write the book you now hold in your hands. I treasured his suggestion and wondered if it would ever become a reality...thank God it has.

I thank our heavenly Father for Suzanne Haffamier, for her exuberance about this book, her sense of humor, and her helpful first edit of the manuscript. We are both Dodger fans to the core.

I am grateful for Bahram Khayatpour for his insight, found in the questions at the close of each chapter.

My deep gratitude also goes to Nadine Erickson, for designing the cover for *The Kairos Adventure*. I always love her artistic touch. I appreciate her creative editing as well. She always makes me look like I know what I am doing.

Thanks to Diane Gardner and Tia Smith for their final edits and proofreading, their helpful suggestions, and their inspiring comments about *The Kairos Adventure*.

My utmost appreciation also goes to Kris Wallen. I thank her so much for enthusiastically accepting my request to publish another book. It is so comforting to know that the whole process is in her capable hands. And thanks to her wonderful husband, Arvid, for taking care of the graphic design on the interior and typesetting. His finishing touches make the book come alive for the reader.

A Tribute to Lyle Randles

When a believer catches the significance of the Great Commandment—loving God and loving neighbors—he or she can't go back to the old way of living. This was certainly true for my dear friend Lyle Randles. Once the Lord showed him that this was what He was up to in our day, Lyle never looked back. He began to pray for his neighbors, care for them, and show them the love of God.

Because of this common love for God and our neighbors, Lyle and I were inseparable. We saw how far the Lord's Church had drifted from this great command of God. We talked about what the Church would look like if it laid aside its human pursuits to grow the Church and instead pursued what Jesus commanded us to do, so He could build His Church. The result is found in the book we co-wrote, *The Incarnational Church: Catching Jesus' Radical Approach for Advancing His Kingdom.* Lyle and I connected daily, either in person, by phone, by text, or by e-mail. I would often be greeted in the morning by a text from him. We shared our excitement together about what God was doing. I remember the day he came into my office and said, "I have good news, and I have bad news." I don't remember what the good news was, but the bad news was that I needed to write another book. *The Kairos Adventure* is the fulfillment of his suggestion.

One afternoon, Lyle sent a text asking if I could take a call from him. I said I couldn't. I was watching my son coach a high school basketball game, but I would call him back afterward. I called after the game, but there was no answer. I received a text the next morning from his wife, Sharon, that Lyle had passed away. I screamed with shock because there was no real warning that something like that was imminent. My dear friend had entered the gates of glory where everyone loves God and loves their neighbor perfectly. I am looking forward to that day when Lyle will show me around the celestial neighborhoods.

Until that day, I will carry on the work the Lord gave us here. But I deeply miss my friend, his incredible contribution to the neighboring movement, his profound influence with pastors and leaders in helping them understand God's heart for His Great Commandment, his personal encouragement, and most of all, his sensitivity to what Daddy was doing.

Introduction to the Adventure

Welcome to *The Kairos Adventure*! You are embarking on a journey filled with surprising and life-changing opportunities to partner with God in the neighborhood. All great adventures begin with excitement and anticipation, and this one is no different. The Lord is about to take you on an adventure better than any ride you will ever experience at any theme park, chock-full of all those same feelings of dread and exhilaration.

You are about to read the stories of people whose worlds were rocked by what God did in their own neighborhoods. Each story actually happened to real people in real neighborhoods. In some cases, you will hear firsthand from people who penned their own story. In other cases, I will share someone else's neighborhood adventure, with their permission, of course, or share one of my own. Each one is intended to open your eyes to how God worked in the lives of people in their neighborhoods and to help you realize that He is doing the same with people in yours. Then we'll consider how you can have eyes to see what God is up to with your neighbors, which is crucial for embarking upon your new adventure.

The anecdotes will allow you to learn from others' experiences and help you better relate to and care for the people in your own neighborhood. Each story will be coupled with an insight drawn from that neighborhood experience followed by an opportunity to reflect and respond.

If you have already read *Neighborhood Initiative and the Love of God* or *The Incarnational Church: Catching Jesus' Radical Approach for Advancing His Kingdom*, you may recognize a few of the stories. Use the reflection time to allow these stories to take shape in your life in a new way as you would a scripture you've read many times before. Stories are powerful. Jesus often taught using them, knowing that stories draw people in. Think about how many lectures or sermons you remember compared to how many stories you recall from those same gifted speakers. The stories in Scripture offer us a glimpse of people being used by God that we can both learn from and use to help others.

Perhaps you too have shared your own stories with others to demonstrate how God used you or with the hope that others would learn from your mistakes. The stories in this book detail authentic divine encounters as well as the struggles that accompany walking out the command to love our neighbors.

You will find that by living the *kairos* life, experiencing divine appointments with God, you don't need to try to make something happen in your neighborhood. God wants to invite you into what He is already doing in your neighbors' lives. It takes the burden off you and allows you to wear the easy yoke (Matthew 11:29–30) with Jesus as you love and care for those around you. You will learn to live the kind of life Jesus did when He loved and cared for those near to Him. Jesus loved His neighbors perfectly and invites you to join Him in doing the same with your neighbors.

Chapter 1 is critical to embarking on your adventure. It is intended to open your eyes to how God worked in the lives of those sharing their stories. To get the most out of *The Kairos Adventure* I encourage you to read one chapter a day and then take time throughout the day to reflect on what the person learned through his or her experience. Though you may not relate to every story, you will see where God was moving in both the protagonist of each adventure and the neighbors encountered. Allow God to shape how He wants you to move in your neighborhood. He may have you try some of the examples laid out here or bring creative new ideas to mind. Enjoy the journey!

1

Having Eyes for the Kairos Adventure

My Father is always at his work to this very day, and I too am working….Very truly I tell you, the Son can do nothing by himself; he can do only what he sees his Father doing, because whatever the Father does the Son also does. For the Father loves the Son and shows him all he does. Yes, and he will show him even greater works than these. —John 5:17, 19, 20

The most exciting life you can experience is the *kairos* life, filled with adventure and surprises. Once you enter this kind of life, you will never wish to go back to the old way of living. It is how Jesus lived His life.

Most of us are driven by the clock, busy lives, and deadlines, but Jesus lived His life free from such constraints. His relationship with His Father and loving and serving people were at the heart of what allowed Him to live a *kairos* life.

Kairos versus Chronos Living

You are probably asking, "What is *kairos*?" I am glad you asked! The Greek language has two words for time: *chronos* and *kairos*. *Chronos* concerns chronological time, as in the twenty-four-hour day. We define our workweeks by the number of hours we work. We create a list of things to do and have only so much time to get everything done. Having a *chronos* mind-set can often make us miss seeing what God is doing all around us. Instead, our eyes are fixed on the clock, where we need to go next, and on checking another item off our to-do-list. We are "asleep" to what God is doing with us and others in the moment.

Kairos is quite different from *chronos*. It is not linear or bound by time constraints in that it doesn't involve a clock or a schedule. It is life lived in the moment. It is being fully present when you are with others. *Kairos* is best referred to as an "opportunity." For example, parents have only a certain season of time to raise their children and then the opportunity is over. Opportunity may refer to either a lengthy period of *chronos* or the short *kairos* moments that we are to redeem. The apostle Paul said, "Wake up, sleeper, rise from the dead, and Christ will shine on you. Be very careful, then, how you live—not as unwise but as wise, making the most of every opportunity [*kairos*]" (Ephesians 5:14–16). And again, he said in Colossians 4:5, "Be wise in the way you act toward outsiders; make the most of every opportunity [*kairos*]." I believe Paul was giving us a window into how he lived his life with those outside the church.

Marcy's Story

A perfect example of a *kairos* moment is when my wife, jo, and I were hosting a Christmas dinner in our home for some people from our church. As people began arriving, I noticed jo at the front door talking with our neighbor Marcy.

Marcy's car had been broken into near her kids' school, and her purse and a great deal of cash had been stolen. She had to freeze her accounts at the bank, leaving her without easy access to emergency funds. Her husband was out of town on business and wouldn't return until the following day. Here she was, just before Christmas, thirty-eight weeks pregnant and home alone with two young children. She was deeply concerned that whoever broke into her car, knowing that she had this amount of cash, would come into our neighborhood, and she came to warn us. She was visibly shaken from the break-in, and jo asked if it would be okay if she prayed for her. Marcy agreed, and jo put her hands on Marcy's shoulders and prayed. As jo prayed, the Lord told me, in a way that only He can communicate, *Give her two hundred dollars.*

After everyone had left our dinner party, jo approached me and said, "How much are we going to give Marcy?" I immediately responded, "The Lord told me two hundred dollars."

I had been to the ATM the day before and had two hundred dollars in my wallet. I asked jo to get a Christmas card ready and said I would go and see if Marcy was still awake. She was still awake, and I gave her the card with the gift inside.

The next day, I got a call from Marcy. She thought I had given her just a Christmas card and had put it on her nightstand with all the others. She woke that morning and decided to read all of her Christmas cards, hoping to cheer herself up. After opening our card, she called me in great surprise, promising to pay me back. I replied, "No, Marcy, that's a gift from God for you." Her response was priceless: "That's not normal!"

I love not being normal.

When I talked to Marcy's husband the following week, he told me that when Marcy told him about the gift he almost cried.

Kairos Moments Require a Choice

Like our story with Marcy, *kairos* moments frequently occur when we least expect them, and they seldom fit into our self-determined plan for the day. They are often viewed as intrusions in our lives. Each time one occurs, we are forced to choose: Do I disrupt my plans and lay them aside for the sake of what God is doing in the moment? Or, do I continue with what I am doing?

I have often thought that when Jesus told the Parable of the Good Samaritan, He was comparing the way He lived His life with the way the religious leaders of His day lived theirs. The priest and the Levite were too busy after their temple service activities to stop and care for their desperate "neighbor" who was beaten and robbed and left to die by the side of the road. Oddly enough, Jesus used a member of the most despised group in society in that day, the Samaritan, to demonstrate extraordinary "neighbor-love." The religious leaders missed out on the *kairos* moment. Helping may have been an inconvenience. They may have been late in getting home, or perhaps there was too much risk involved. They could not be bothered.

Doing What the Father Is Doing

You may be asking now, "How do I move from seeing these moments as more than impositions and enter into the *kairos* life?" During the early development of Neighborhood Initiative, the Lord helped me understand that there were two ways I could choose to move forward with this good work that He initiated: I could try to make things happen on my own or I could join Him in what He was doing. This is at the heart of the *kairos* lifestyle. I discovered the first approach was difficult and frustrating, because I was trying to make things happen.

The second approach was easy and full of wonderful surprises because God was inviting me into what He was already doing. I found this to be true in my own neighborhood. If I wanted to see God's kingdom move, then I needed to relinquish my good intentions and plans and surrender my will to the work that He was already doing with those in my neighborhood. It was a revelation for someone who had, for years in ministry, relied on developing a strategy to reach people with the gospel. It was so freeing to rely on God to lead me into relationship with those in my neighborhood.

I was experiencing what Jesus spoke of when He said, "Take my yoke upon you and learn from me, for I am gentle and humble in heart, and you will find rest for your souls. For my yoke is easy and my burden is light" (Matthew 11:29–30). Many people in our time and culture are unfamiliar with what a yoke is. A yoke is a wooden crosspiece that is fastened over the necks of two animals and attached to the plow or cart that they are to pull to make sure they are moving in the same direction. When yoked, one animal establishes dominance over the other and in doing so sets the pace for the two and takes more of the weight. I learned that it was Jesus who was leading and carrying the heavy weight, and I was joining Him in the easy yoke. He took away the burden and any sense of guilt in serving God in my neighborhood.

"DON'T EVER TRY TO MAKE ANYTHING HAPPEN."

In the early days of Neighborhood Initiative, Dallas Willard, a dear friend and well-known philosophy professor at the University of Southern California, told me, "Don't stop doing what you are doing. If you keep moving forward with what you are doing, we will see revival and awakening." These were significant words coming from Dallas, a man who walked closely with Jesus and was deeply respected by many Christian leaders, and someone who chose his words carefully. I took what he said to heart.

If you have listened to Dallas or read much of his teaching, you know one of his noteworthy quotes is, "Don't ever try to make anything happen." I watched this up close and personal in his life. He didn't need to promote himself or try to make things happen, yet God used him greatly to influence so many lives in and outside the church. He understood and lived in the "easy yoke" with Jesus and did what the Father was doing. By this yoking with the Lord, Dallas was in one accord with Him.

Joining What the Father Is Doing

Not trying to make something happen is such a freeing way to live life. I have found three things I can do that enable me to live a life free of performance and of "trying to make something happen."

These three simple activities have allowed me to see what the Father is doing and then, after His invitation, join Him. They have shown me His activity in my own neighborhood, empowered me to live the *kairos* life, and allowed me to seize divine opportunities: I pray, and I wait, and I watch.

I Pray

You probably pray in a set way. I would encourage you to stay with the way the Lord has directed you. I believe prayer, conversing with God and Him with you, is a personal matter…there is no one way to do it. In this season of my life, prayer walking has become most refreshing for me. It allows me to zero in as I listen and talk with my Father. Each day of the week, I walk and pray with a different focus in mind. On Tuesday mornings, I walk through my neighborhood and *I pray* for each of my neighbors by name. I ask the Lord to show me what He is doing in their lives. Sometimes He will speak to me about my neighbors or give me ideas of what He would like me to do. Other times I hear nothing or see nothing happening and have boldly asked Him, "Is this a fruitless activity?" Like in Marcy's story, He has faithfully and dramatically shown me that He is in favor of my weekly prayer walks in my neighborhood. So, I have continued to make them my regular practice.

I Wait

Rather than rushing ahead to make something happen in my neighborhood, after I pray, *I wait* for Him. This kind of waiting is not a passive waiting, but a waiting with a sense of expectation. When Isaiah spoke of "those who wait on the LORD" in Isaiah

40:31 (NKJV), he was referring to a waiting with expectation, and that's the kind of waiting I do. I would add, expectation does not imply that I wait for what I believe will happen, but rather that I know He will continue to lead the way. *I pray* and then *I wait* for the next thing the Father invites me to do with Him in my neighborhood.

I have been prayer walking through our present neighborhood for years. I must confess, in the early days, I sometimes questioned if anything would ever happen in our neighborhood. Most of us have a tendency to want to make something happen, like a child who wants to force open a budding flower before its time. But if you pray and wait, God is faithful and begins to open the hearts of people in your neighborhood like He opens a flower to display its beauty in its proper time and season.

I Watch

Then *I watch*, and out of nowhere something will happen that I least expect. A neighbor will call me and ask me to perform a wedding at his home, or another will ask me to officiate at a funeral for someone in the neighborhood. Or a fifty-foot tree is blown down in front of our home, the tree lands on our neighbor's house across the street, a car is crushed, and an opportunity opens up with a neighbor. Or I follow an ambulance up the street, and the experience opens a new relationship with one of my neighbors. You can't control, anticipate, or predict these things; however, because of God's sovereign working and prayer, He has invited me in to participate in His ongoing work.

Patiently waiting and watching for God to do His work in your neighbors' lives can, at times, become discouraging and may cause us to lose heart because we don't see results immediately. We want the work to take place in our timing. We might even find ourselves trying to make something happen in our neighbors' lives to hurry the process along. "The Garden," a children's story from the Frog and Toad series, gives a helpful parable for us who are impatient with this process. Here's a summary of the story:

> When Toad sees Frog's beautiful garden, Toad decides that he too would like to have a garden. Frog tells Toad that a garden is hard work and gives Toad some flower seeds to plant. After Toad plants the seeds, he tells them to start growing, and when they do not do so immediately, he shouts to the ground that the seeds should start growing—but this still doesn't work. Frog suggests that Toad is frightening the seeds with all the shouting and tells Toad to leave the seeds alone for a few days.
>
> That night Toad observes that the seeds have still not begun to grow, and he worries that they are afraid of the dark. Toad begins experimenting with reading stories and poems to the seeds and playing music for them. Still, the seeds do not grow. Eventually, Toad falls asleep, and when he wakes up he sees that the seeds have started to grow. He is very happy that his "seeds have stopped being afraid to grow." Toad then reports to Frog that Frog was right, growing a garden is "very hard work."[1]

The Frog and Toad story helps us better understand what Jesus conveyed in the Parable of the Growing Seed. "This is what the kingdom of God is like. A man scatters seed on the ground. Night and day, whether he sleeps or gets up, the seed sprouts and grows, though he does not know how. All by itself the soil produces grain—first the stalk, then the head, then the full kernel in the head. As soon as the grain is ripe, he puts the sickle to it, because the harvest has come" (Mark 4:26–29). Often, the process with neighbors is slow. But one day, when you least expect it, God surprises you with an invitation to join Him in His work with one of your neighbors, like He has with me on so many occasions.

Becoming Like a Child

Living the *kairos* life with the Father is like being a little kid who is waiting for his dad to invite him on a new excursion. He knows that only Dad can drive the car, and he waits for his dad to say, "Come on, kid! I have a wonderful surprise for you. Let's go!" And off they go together with Dad in the driver's seat. This is the adventure I spoke of earlier. This is the *kairos* adventure: becoming like a child and enjoying the ride with Dad on an amazing journey through life with those in your own neighborhood.

A time for reflection

Are you ready to experience the *kairos* life where the Father opens doors for you and you join Him on an amazing adventure? This is where it starts, "Devote yourselves to prayer, being watchful and thankful. And pray for us, too, that God may open a door for our message…Make the most of every opportunity [*kairos*]" (Colossians 4:2–3, 5). Devoting yourself to what the apostle Paul set forth is the door into an incredible life with the Father and to joining Him as He advances His kingdom through you. Are you ready for the adventure? If yes, what would it take to establish this kind of rhythm in your life, a rhythm of devoting yourself to prayer and of being watchful so that you are left with gratitude for what the Father has done?

Respond

What is one thing that was mentioned in the chapter that you can start doing today?

_____

_____

_____

2

Seeing with New Eyes

[Jesus] got up from the meal, took off his outer clothing, and wrapped a towel around his waist. After that, he poured water into a basin and began to wash his disciples' feet, drying them with the towel that was wrapped around him....When he had finished washing their feet, he put on his clothes and returned to his place. "Do you understand what I have done for you?" he asked them. "You call me 'Teacher' and 'Lord,' and rightly so, for that is what I am. Now that I, your Lord and Teacher, have washed your feet, you also should wash one another's feet. I have set you an example that you should do as I have done for you. Very truly I tell you, no servant is greater than his master, nor is a messenger greater than the one who sent him. Now that you know these things, you will be blessed if you do them."
—John 13:4–5, 12–17

In my book *Neighborhood Initiative and the Love of God*, I share a quote from Dallas Willard that has changed my perspective. He portrayed loving our neighbors in this way: "Deeds of love toward others nearby is exactly the 'washing of feet' that Jesus exemplified and told us to do."[2] Sometimes we get so busy in life and ministry that we overlook the most significant opportunity to "wash" a neighbor's feet. But there are times when the Lord stops us so we can see through all the clutter in our hectic lives. That's when He allows us to see a neighbor's need. It may even be humbling, as it was for Robin Jones Gunn. Observe how her eyes were opened to this reality in her moving story where she refers to herself as "Ministry Woman."

Robin Jones Gunn's Neighborhood

I had a moment in my life, as we all do, when a bit of eternal truth broke through my "convenient Christianity," and I was radically changed.

We lived in a small university town where God opened up many opportunities for ministry. My husband was working as a youth pastor. We had teenagers over to our house all the time and even had a college student living with us. I accepted a part-time position as what they called a "radio personality" at a Christian station in town. I was busy writing a series of teen novels for a Christian publisher, and women's groups were calling asking me to speak at various events. In every way, I was "Ministry Woman"!

One night I was on the phone with my best friend, Donna. In three weeks she and I were to fly to Europe where I'd been invited to speak. There was so much to do, and I told Donna, "If one more person asks for one more little piece of me, I'm going to fall apart! I have no more pieces left to give."

As I was speaking to her, the call waiting signal on my phone started beeping. I ignored it, but the caller continued to dial in. "Just a minute, Donna," I said.

It was almost ten o'clock, and the caller turned out to be my neighbor Jana. She said, "Robin, I didn't know who else to call… could you come up? Just for a minute?"

I thought, *Okay. This is it. The last piece of my sanity and now my neighbor wants to take it from me. Doesn't it ever let up?*

I considered saying no. I thought she would certainly understand if I said it was too late. I would come see her in the morning. Whatever it was could wait until then, couldn't it?

"Oh, all right," I heard myself tell Jana. "I'll be there in a minute."

I told Donna I'd have to call her back, and I jerked the front door open, ready to march up the street to Jana's house.

It was a crisp, cold night. It had been snowing. That, and the fact that I walked out without a jacket, made me feel even more inconvenienced. I couldn't imagine what Jana wanted. I'd given her all my books, but she hadn't read them. I'd told her when my radio program aired, but she never listened. I'd given her two books by important Christian psychologists when her husband left her, but she hadn't gotten around to reading them. The way I saw it, I'd done my part. Jana simply wasn't interested in coming to the Lord.

"I SAW WHAT GOD DESIRED OF MY LIFE."

When I arrived at her front door, Jana stood there on crutches. I'd forgotten that she told me a week ago that she was having her right hip replaced. She had now had both hips replaced before she was forty-five due to arthritis. I knew her mom had come from the East Coast the first few days to help out, but her mom had gone home. Her ex-husband had their two daughters every Thursday, and this was Thursday. Jana stood before me, all alone.

"Thanks so much for coming," Jana said, showing me in and

hobbling to the hospital bed set up in the family room. "I didn't know who else to call. You see, I wanted to go to bed, but"— she looked down at her feet—"I couldn't take off my shoes."

In that moment, I realized that I thought I was "Ministry Woman," and yet I was not worthy to untie the laces on my neighbor's tennis shoes.

I knelt down, and let me tell you, it was all I could do to not wash her feet with my tears. I saw what God desired of my life. I suddenly understood His concept of ministry. All God has asked me to do is love Him and love my neighbor.

That's what a real ministry woman does.

I untied Jana's shoes and slipped them off her feet. Then I helped her take off her sweatpants. I saw the scar. It was vile. *So much pain*, I thought. *And no one here to comfort you.*

Jana slid into bed, but I didn't want to leave just because my task was done. I pulled the comforter up to her chin and asked if she'd like a cup of cold water.

I brought one for her. *In Jesus' name*, I thought, as she sipped from the glass tumbler.

Then before I could be self-conscious about what she might think of me, I kissed her on the cheek and said, "Good night, Jana. I love you."

"I know," she said. "That's why I called you. I knew you would come."

A year and a half later, Jana gave her life to the Lord. We had moved to another state when she told me her good news on the phone. She was excited about her plans to go on the woman's retreat and join the weekly Bible study group at the church she was attending.

More than once I have wondered what would have happened if I had said no on that snowy night. After all, I had books to write, planes to catch, and a radio show to record in the morning. What if I had missed the opportunity for the pure and undefiled ministry of loving my neighbor simply because I was too caught up in my own version of being "Ministry Woman"?

A time for reflection

One of the most difficult things for us busy Christians to do is to create margin in our lives for God moments...divine appointments. Some of us, like Robin, are so busy that if one more person asks one more thing of us, we too are going to fall apart. We need to bring our busy schedules before the Lord and ask Him what is really important in our daily life. We need to ask the question, How can I create margin in my life so that I have time for my neighbors? More importantly, we need to ask, How can I have more time for God? Not only time alone with Him, but time for Him throughout the day when He calls on us to care for a neighbor's need. It sounds simple enough, but it can be challenging when we realize this means actually saying no to something we think is more important. What is your schedule like, and how could you simplify your life to make room for life as God intended it? What change(s) could you make?

Respond

Make a list of your neighbors' needs. You can identify a need through conversation with them or just from seeing them from afar. For example, does your neighbor's home need painting, tree need trimming, etc.? Maybe your neighbors are always busy with the kids and need a meal.

_____

_____

_____

_____

_____

_____

_____

_____

Robin Jones Gunn is the much-loved author of the popular Christy Miller series for teens and Sisterchicks® novels as well as non-fiction favorites such as Victim of Grace *and* Spoken For. *Her ninety books have sold nearly five million copies worldwide. Robin is a frequent speaker at local and international events. She and her husband live in Hawaii where she continues to write her heart out. For more information go to www.robingunn.com.*

3

An Eye-Opening Moment

But to you who are listening I say: Love your enemies, do good to those who hate you, bless those who curse you, pray for those who mistreat you. If someone slaps you on one cheek, turn to them the other also. If someone takes your coat, do not withhold your shirt from them. Give to everyone who asks you, and if anyone takes what belongs to you, do not demand it back. Do to others as you would have them do to you. — Luke 6:27–31

We all have one or two neighbors challenge us in our neighborhoods. Jesus' statement here by all means seems counterintuitive when a neighbor is testing us to the nth degree. We sarcastically ask, "Love *them*? Do good to *them*? Bless *them*? Pray for *them*? Come on now! You have got to be kidding me!" When we read what Jesus said here when all is going well with our neighbors, it seems well and good, but try applying this when tensions rise between you and a neighbor. Brian's story will make you laugh, but see how hard it was for him to apply what Jesus said in these verses. Let's learn from his life lesson.

Brian and Julie Mavis's Neighborhood

Our neighbor, I'll call him Joe, easily had the best yard on the block. Joe was in his yard all the time, tending to his super-green grass with nothing out of place. He gave me advice like, "This is what you ought to do." "Use this weed killer." "Water this way." "Use this turf builder." I appreciated his advice, and it seemed like we were getting along. But then I noticed how obsessed he was with his yard. He had cut down every tree on his property so he wouldn't have leaves. He mowed almost every day. When he got done mowing, he would use scissors to trim the whole yard. (I am not exaggerating.) That's when I thought we might have a problem.

Joe's advice and encouragement turned into criticism, and he started getting frustrated with my gardening skills. It turned insulting, actually, and finally got to the point where we couldn't even talk to or look at each other. It progressed to the point that I wouldn't go outside if he was outside. I would check to make sure Joe wasn't there. It was bad. For about a year I tried to avoid Joe, my neighbor, at all cost.

Fast forward a couple of years, and Julie and I have two daughters, ages three and one. Joe, among other criticisms, warned me about letting my girls walk around barefoot. He was angry that we had a tree, and leaves from it would occasionally fall or blow into his yard. He would collect the leaves that got into his yard, bag them up, and dump them back into our yard.

"IN AN INSTANT I WAS PRAYING WITH HIM."

One evening we were all outside cleaning up the leaves in the yard. We didn't have a sprinkler system, so my wife started watering the yard with a hose. My oldest daughter was next to Julie as she accidently splashed some water onto Joe's driveway.

Joe blew a gasket. He ran up to Julie and started shouting at her for splashing water onto his driveway. On the other side of the yard, I wondered what I should do. I'm a pastor, a man of God. So I did what you'd expect: I ran over and shoved him away from Julie. I pinned him against his truck, and we yelled at each other like an umpire and a manager at home plate.

During our argument, I learned just how fixated he was about our little girls walking around barefoot. He had placed broken glass in our yard just to teach us a lesson.

Joe was nuts, and I was ready to crack his shell.

I didn't punch him or throw him to the ground, but I did about everything else. After we had been screaming at each other for about twenty minutes, I realized I was out of control. I stormed into the house, exasperated, and asked Julie, "What are we going to do with this guy?"

She got all spiritual on me. "Maybe we ought to pray for him," she said.

All right! Let's pray for Seal Team Six to take him out! I thought.

For about a week we prayed for him, and we prayed for us. In my prayers I heard God say, *You need to apologize.*

I fought it, telling God, "No way! This guy is wrong, not me."

God kept pressing in: *You need to make things right.*

My response was always no.

About a week later I peeked out to see if I could leave my house without bumping into Joe. With the coast clear, I grabbed my stuff and opened the door. At the same time, Joe stepped out of his house.

That's the problem with prayer. It makes things happen, sometimes whether we like it or not. I felt like I was seeing a girl for the first time after a bad breakup.

We stared at each other and then approached each other. Simultaneously we said to each other, "I am so sorry."

We both apologized, knowing we shouldn't have argued in the way that we had. We apologized not just for that incident, but for the year prior and the tension of not talking to each other.

Joe said, "Let's make things right." We had never had a spiritual conversation up to that point, but he said, "I know you're a pastor, and I'd like to talk to you about God."

I was shocked. What the heck was happening? After a year of trying to stay out of this guy's way, in an instant I was praying with him.[3]

(Brian's story is from *The Neighboring Church: Getting Better at What Jesus Said Matters Most* by Rick Rusaw and Brian Mavis.)

A time for reflection

Needless to say, this situation got way out of hand. But the turning point was when Julie came out with, "Maybe we ought to pray for him." Brian experienced real tension with this suggestion. Can you imagine what thoughts were going through Brian's head when, after that week of prayer, he heard God tell him to apologize? Brian experienced a *kairos* moment when he and Joe met face-to-face. Time stood still as hearts were humbled and everything changed.

Brian's words are so true: "That's the problem with prayer. It makes things happen, sometimes whether we like it or not." Do you have a difficult neighbor or someone that you need to pray for or bless or do something good for? Today would be a good day to start by bringing this person before the Lord and asking Him what you could do to show love to this neighbor.

✍ Respond

In what way is this neighbor difficult for you, and how can you consistently be praying for him or her?

_____

_____

_____

_____

_____

Brian is the president of America's Kids Belong, a nonprofit that exists to empower leaders in the government, faith-based, business, and creative sectors to end the crisis for kids in foster care—state by state. Brian challenges leaders to solve big problems and encourages Christians to live a better expression of their faith. Brian helped build and lead SermonCentral.com in its early years. He has written curriculum and sermons for national campaigns including Bono's One Sabbath Campaign, Mel Gibson's movie The Passion of the Christ, World Vision's Faith in Action, *and the book* The Hole in Our Gospel.

4

Listening for the Lord's Voice

My sheep listen to my voice; I know them, and they
follow me. —John 10:27

Some time ago, I was rooming at a conference with a pastor friend
from Oxford, England. He had two degrees from Oxford. One,
believe it or not, was in shepherding. The last day we were together, I asked, "Could you tell me something about shepherd and
sheep? I want to have something to remember about our time
together." He paused and then said, "It's true that sheep do listen
to the shepherd's voice." He went on to tell me that when other
family members of the shepherd approach the sheep, the sheep do
not respond like they do to him. He said if the sheep even see his
silhouette against an early-morning sunrise, they come running.
Hearing and obeying our Shepherd's voice is so important as we
love our neighbor, as you will learn from Debi Smith Wineroth's
story.

Debi Smith Wineroth's Neighborhood

I was upstairs in my two-story townhouse ironing. I thought, *I
need to get a lamp for this corner of the room. It's too dark.* I put it on
my mental to-do list.

A couple of days later I was getting ready to go for a run. It
was wintertime, and it had been raining a lot, so I peeked outside

to the parking lot area to see if the ground was wet so I could dress appropriately. To my surprise, I observed a man going through our community dumpster. I was immediately upset that this was going on just outside my back patio. I marched downstairs to get the phone number for the local police block watch. There was a substation right on my property where the police used to do their paperwork.

I found the phone number, and as I reached for my phone I clearly heard God say, *It looks to Me like he could use a hot cup of coffee.* I said, "WHAAATTTT? You've got to be kidding!" Then God said, *And take him a couple of those homemade cookies you've got over there on the counter.* Well, I didn't like the idea one bit, but there was no denying the voice of God. As I pulled out my coffee maker, ground some fresh beans, and began the brewing process, I kept looking out my patio door, hoping that he would be gone before the coffee was ready. No such luck! So there I went...out through my patio gate with a mug of coffee in one hand and a plate of cookies in the other.

"YOU'D BE SURPRISED HOW OFTEN PEOPLE DON'T LISTEN."

He was kneeling down sorting through his pile of treasures as I approached. I briefly noticed that he had quite an accumulation of items both big and small, and I had a fleeting thought: *How does he transport all that stuff?* As I drew closer, he looked up and saw me coming. His head dropped in shame, knowing that he was about to get kicked off the property. I walked up to him and said, "Good morning. God told me that you could use a cup of coffee…and some cookies." Again, his head dropped and slowly shook back and forth in disbelief. He slowly stood up, and I found myself looking into the beautiful clear blue eyes of a young man.

He thanked me, while slowly removing his gloves, and took the coffee and cookies. He told me about all the valuable things he finds that people throw away. He pointed to his pile of treasures, and again I wondered how he transported them. We talked for a while, and then I said, "I'm going for a run. That's my townhouse over there. When you're done you can put the mug and the plate on my wall, and I'll get it when I return." He thanked me again and said, "It was nice talking to you. You'd be surprised how often people don't listen. God bless you." I said, "Oh, He does; thank you."

When I returned from my run, sitting up on my wall was the mug; the plate; and a beautiful, well-polished, imitation Tiffany lamp. That lamp now lights up my dark corner.

Looking back and thinking about the man's parting words—"You'd be surprised how often people don't listen"—I realize now that he wasn't talking about listening to him. He was talking about listening to HIM, the voice of God.

Thank You, Father, that on that particular day I heard Your voice and was obedient, because I got to have an encounter with one of Your angels.

A time for reflection

The writer of Hebrew stated, "Do not forget to show hospitality to strangers, for by so doing some people have shown hospitality to angels without knowing it" (Hebrews 13:2). At the time, Debi didn't realize whom she was entertaining, but it became quite evident that this young man was sent by God to speak to her. God speaks to us in a variety of ways, and when He does, it is best to obey His voice as Debi did.

Has the Lord ever made some unusual request like this of you with a neighbor? How did you respond to Him? Did you follow through with His request? If you did, how did it impact you and your neighbor? Can you recall a time you didn't respond to an inner prompting? Don't beat yourself up. This too can be a valuable growth opportunity to help you distinguish the different ways God speaks to you so you can recognize Him as He continues to speak to you.

Respond

What has God shared with you about your neighborhood?

_____

_____

_____

_____

After thirty years as a flight attendant, Debi Smith Wineroth retired and moved from Phoenix, Arizona, to Chico, California, to become a full-time volunteer with Youth With A Mission (YWAM). She found her love for missions work while vacationing in Mexico. During that trip God presented an opportunity for her to serve in the poorest communities, and while doing that she realized that she'd found her calling. In her retirement years, her traveling continues, but as a YWAMer she is "serving" in a totally different way.

5

A Modern-Day
Good Samaritan

A man was going down from Jerusalem to Jericho, when he was attacked by robbers. They stripped him of his clothes, beat him and went away, leaving him half dead. A priest happened to be going down the same road, and when he saw the man, he passed by on the other side. So too, a Levite, when he came to the place and saw him, passed by on the other side. But a Samaritan, as he traveled, came where the man was; and when he saw him, he took pity on him. He went to him and bandaged his wounds, pouring on oil and wine. Then he put the man on his own donkey, brought him to an inn and took care of him. The next day he took out two denarii and gave them to the innkeeper. "Look after him," he said, "and when I return, I will reimburse you for any extra expense you may have." Which of these three do you think was a neighbor to the man who fell into the hands of robbers?
—Luke 10:30–36

I have read the story of the Good Samaritan often and thought of it as just what it is…a story to encourage us to love our neighbor. Though this is true, there is something much deeper here. After looking closer at this parable Jesus gave to an expert in the law, I have found that Jesus also intended to convey something profound about Himself. If you look closely, you will see that Jesus used the Samaritan, the most despised in society at that time, to portray His ministry in comparison to that of the religious leaders of His day. Jesus was not one to toot His own horn, so He wrapped something about Himself in the story of the Good Samaritan. Jesus was moved with compassion and entered our world, bandaged our wounds, and so on. Jesus concluded His story with these words to the expert in the law: "Go and do likewise." In other words, Jesus was saying, "Go and do what I have done." And that is what Nadine Erickson did with someone at her own front door who was in a similar condition to the man on the side of the road. Here's her story.

Nadine Erickson's Neighborhood

I awoke to the doorbell ringing. I glanced at the clock, saw 2:00 a.m., and figured my mom had forgotten her key. My four children and I live with her, so it seemed the only thing that made sense at that hour. What followed was a pounding at the front door and a woman's screams. I ran to the front and peered through the shutters to see a young woman in distress looking the other way yelling, "Please help me, somebody! Please!"

The teenager who lives next door is troubled, and it wasn't uncommon to see the police at her place. My immediate thought was that she was in trouble again. There was no question about opening the door to her. But then the visitor turned toward me, and I didn't recognize the bloody face looking my way. You'd think I had seen enough violent movies to be unfazed by this scene, but this was the real thing. It sent a chill up my spine.

In the span of a few seconds I realized that this was a stranger, and if I chose to open the door, who knows what I would be letting inside. My impulse to help had already taken over and overpowered my fear. I quickly brought her in, looked around outside to see if other people were there, and then locked her safely inside with me and my family. My unholy thoughts turned to where to let her sit down. I determined she would ruin the sofa with all the blood, so I had her sit on an upholstered chair next to the front door as I made a quick assessment of her situation.

Dark blood ran from a couple of stab wounds on her neck. She wore a short plaid skirt, and she had a lot of tattoos for a young girl. I thought of my own daughters and judgment arose. She had obviously been no stranger to late nights without supervision. She cried, "I'm bleeding. I don't want to die!"

I tried to calm her saying, "You are safe. I am going to call for help." The 911 operator had me question the girl for details. Even as frightened as the injured girl was, her answers were vague, and she avoided saying who was responsible. My mom was awakened by all of the commotion and helped me put pressure on the more serious wounds.

About six police officers arrived and set to questioning her again. Unfortunately, they obtained little more information than the 911 operator received. They removed her shirt to assess the damage, and I was surprised at how many more stab wounds she had on her back, wrist, stomach, and sides. I really wasn't needed beyond providing extra towels, but I stayed close and told her I was proud of her and what a brave girl she was. All the while I was asking God if I shouldn't be doing something more, as if this were the perfect opportunity to use me in some grand act of healing, but I didn't hear any prompting.

"REMEMBER WHEN YOU THOUGHT IT WAS THE NEIGHBOR GIRL?"

So many miracles occurred that evening. First, her life was spared and there were no repercussions to inviting her inside. Secondly, my six- and seven-year-old boys sleep in that same front room with only a room divider separating their space. Despite the girl's screams and the officers loudly questioning her, they remained asleep. None of us were being particularly quiet. My daughters sleep in the bedroom right next to the front room with a window facing the front of the house. They slept through most of the activities as well, and by the time my oldest had determined she shouldn't miss this once-in-a-lifetime chance to see what was going on, the paramedics had covered the girl with a sheet so there would be no violent image to haunt her thoughts.

The officers, detectives, and forensic people filtered through over the next several hours. One flat-out told me I did the wrong thing by letting her in; several others said I was a Good Samaritan and that I had saved her life. I learned the girl was twenty years old and in a gang. My mother, a little traumatized by the incident, didn't like my decision. I took it all in.

Blood was splattered all over the front of the door, the porch, the floor, and the walls. And yes, the upholstery on that chair was ruined. After my mom and I finished off the bottle of hydrogen peroxide cleaning up, I sat in a bath soaking in the fears I had repressed and cried out to God, "What was I thinking? It could have gone so differently. I put my family in danger. Did I do the wrong thing?"

I heard God break through my heavy thoughts with, *Remember when you thought it was the neighbor girl? That was Me. There wasn't time for more. I needed you to know it was OK.*

Sometime later an officer told me that the girl finally agreed to testify against the gang members that attacked her and dumped her across the street from my house. Apparently, she had witnessed a murder, and they were trying to keep her quiet.

A year later I was coming back from a run and noticed three young people parked across the street from my house looking at me. They were obviously staring, so I asked if I could help them. The girl approached. It was her. She wanted to thank me. She said she knew she was given another chance and she was trying to live a better life, but I smelled the alcohol on her and knew she was still finding her way. She showed me her wrist where there was nerve damage from one of the stab wounds, but she was grateful to be alive. I told her again that I was proud of her. She swore that the porch light was on that night and that's why she headed my way even though she had been dumped a house or two away from mine. We never leave the light on, but I have no doubt that she saw a light. To be honest, I don't always want to have my recognizable light on. It's almost always inconvenient to be available to those who need help. But the reward of knowing I partnered with God for a moment feels pretty amazing.

A time for reflection

The first responders in Nadine's story had two different responses to her opening the door to this young woman—one was negative and the other was positive, that she was a Good Samaritan. Jesus certainly pointed out in the story of the Good Samaritan that there will be risk in loving our neighbor. We could conclude from the first responders' feedback that there are only two ways to respond to a situation like Nadine's: avoid it at all costs or risk everything for the sake of the one in need. However, there is a third option, as Nadine points out in her story. Can you find the *kairos* moment in her story? The Lord was the one who arranged everything in her story to save this young woman's life. How sensitive are you to the Spirit's leading in the moment?

Respond

What would lead you to a greater sensitivity to the Lord's prompting?

_____

_____

_____

_____

Nadine works as a contractor in a variety of fields including teaching, interpreting Spanish, graphic design, and music. She and her four children live in the San Fernando Valley. Nadine has been an incredible support to me with Neighborhood Initiative since its inception. She designed the covers of my three books and helped me write Neighborhood Initiative and the Love of God *and* The Kairos Adventure. *Most of all, I am indebted to her heart for this good work and the camaraderie we have shared through the years.*

6

Do I Have to Love My Neighbor?

Now he had to go through Samaria. —John 4:4

The story of Jesus meeting the woman at the well is a favorite, but it begins with an unusual statement: "Now he had to go through Samaria." This reflected Jewish thinking of Jesus' day: *I will only go through Samaria if I have to. Samaritans might be our neighbors, but they are to be avoided. It was an "Us versus Them" mentality. If I have to go through Samaria, I will do it quickly and with minimal contact.* In John 4:27, the disciples were astonished when they found Jesus engaged in a long conversation (the longest conversation recorded in the Gospels) with a woman with strange beliefs and loose morals.

Bill and Anamarie Dwyer

I (Bill) hate to admit it, but for years, like many Christians, I avoided my neighbors. When I say "*avoid*" I don't mean I didn't care about their lives or salvation. I just mean I didn't stop long enough to engage them. I would wave. I might even chat over the hedge. But I wasn't intentional about relating to them. We never had long conversations. Instead, I focused on my relationships at church, where I was surrounded by people who had common values and beliefs. I enjoyed a great sense of community in my church, but I had almost no sense of community in the community where I lived. The neighbors I loved were all Christians, and they loved me.

When my wife and I moved to Northridge, California, the Lord put it on our hearts to be intentional with our neighbors. The first thing we did (actually, she did) was to host an open house. Anamarie went door-to-door giving out handmade invitations to our dessert get-together. We were shocked when over thirty people showed up, many with bottles of wine.

Many of our neighbors had never met, even though they had lived here for decades. Some told us they were surprised to see our next-door neighbor. They thought she was dead! It was a diverse group ethnically, spiritually, and socially. We discovered a number of our neighbors were believers, but we realized, like us, they had little relationship with the people on our street. They were too busy with family and church.

"I'M THE NEIGHBOR, AND I'M HERE TO HELP."

Our little soiree confirmed the Lord's leading, so we began inviting neighbors to our small group. Not all responded, but several did, and one at a time they opened their hearts to Jesus. One precious neighbor, Lola, who gave her life to Christ, died a few years ago. We were at her side as she was in hospice at home. Knowing she is with the Lord is just wonderful.

I decided to become more intentional about being available in crisis situations. Our neighborhood had several elderly shut-ins who frequently fell. Weekly the paramedics rolled down our street with flashing lights. The local fire captain even whispered to me, "We call your neighborhood, 'The Legends of the Fall.'"

When an emergency vehicle showed up, I noticed that neighbors gathered and stood around trying to figure out what happened. I tried a different approach. I simply walked into the home like I belonged there and humbly declared, "I'm the neighbor, and I'm here to help." Although the paramedics looked at me like I was a bit strange, my neighbors always appreciated me being there, even if I barely knew them. When serious injuries occurred, I was able to hold hands, give a hug, pray, or provide a ride to a family member who needed to follow the ambulance to the hospital. People open up in crises, and important bonds form as you simply make yourself available.

On one occasion, the fire department, paramedics, police, and coroner descended on our street. A large crowd gathered. People were wondering what had happened. One woman whispered, "I heard he murdered his wife." Although I didn't know the family, I decided I wasn't just going to stand in the crowd and be a spectator to a tragedy. I ducked under the police tape, walked through the front door, and pulled my, "I'm the neighbor, and I'm here to help" card.

I found a heartbroken husband and father. He had come home with his young son to find his wife had taken her life in their home. I was able to sit with him for quite a while. When I offered prayer, he was very grateful. Many years have passed, but that dad and I remain friends. He has come to Christ, and so has his son. In fact, his boy was active in our Children's Ministry for years. Now a teenager, he recently stopped by my home with a couple of high school friends and said, "Hey, Bill, I want you to meet my buddies. They are Christians, too." It brought Anamarie and I to tears.

A time for reflection

When Jesus called His followers to "love your neighbor," He wasn't giving us an option or suggestion, but a command. That's why Jesus "had to go through Samaria." He had to model not ignoring the people who live next to us. That's why He had to engage an immoral woman with strange beliefs. She needed Living Water to wash her of her sins and satisfy her thirst. Our neighbors need that same Living Water, and God has planted us in neighborhoods throughout our cities so we can share the life of Jesus with others. Take some time to think about and pray about your neighbors. How can you be more intentional with them? If you ask with sincerity, I'm sure the Lord will speak.

Respond

Often it is easier to strike up a conversation when there is a shared interest. Make a list of some things that are happening in your neighborhood that may interest the rest of your neighbors. Pray for God to give you an opportunity to use your new conversation starters with your neighbors.

_____

_____

_____

_____

_____

_____

_____

Bill has been the pastor of the Valley Vineyard in Reseda, California, for forty years and has been privileged to be part of the Vineyard Movement from day one. Lynn Cory was his associate for thirty years and "infected" Bill with a passion for loving his neighbors. Bill is joyfully married to Anamarie, a theater professor at California State University, Northridge. They have seven beloved and cherished grandchildren.

7

Your Home Was Prearranged

> From one man he made all the nations, that they should inhabit the whole earth; and he marked out their appointed times in history and the boundaries of their lands. God did this so that they would seek him and perhaps reach out for him and find him, though he is not far from any one of us. —Acts 17:26–27

The apostle Paul, when speaking the preceding verses at the Areopagus, a bare marble hill next to the Acropolis in Athens, was opposing two schools of thought of the day…Stoical Fate and Epicurean Chance. The Stoics believed that all things were governed by irresistible fate. The Epicureans entirely denied providence and held the world to be the effect of mere chance. Paul contested both, attributing the times and locations in which men live and nations exist to the sovereign will and prearrangements of a living God. Paul claimed that God is always working among people so that they will seek Him and perhaps reach out for Him and find Him because He is not far from any one of us.

God clearly works in people's lives, hoping that they will reach out for Him and find Him. If you look back, you just might find how God arranged everything for you so that you would give your life to Him. It wasn't a matter of chance or fate, but a sovereign God arranging circumstances, perhaps a person or people in your life, and the very location where you would turn your life over to Him. This was true for Natalie. Listen to her story and observe how God arranged everything so that she would reach out to Him.

Natalie Wright-Ruiz's Neighborhood

My neighbors were praying for me before they ever met me. There is no other explanation for what God accomplished in the fullness of His time. Nothing in my life would have caused me to look up but God Himself and the prayers of those neighbors in that cul-de-sac. I hadn't thought of God or considered Him in many years.

I was twenty-four years old and six months into a marriage already in trouble. I recall driving home from work feeling utterly hopeless and depressed. I had never felt more desperate and lost. I turned off my radio and began to pray out loud. I was raised Catholic and knew many rote prayers, but I had never done this before; I talked to God as if He were real and listening just to me. I was raised by wonderful parents and had always loved God and believed in Him, but my religious upbringing hadn't led me to any kind of a personal relationship with Him. The tears coursed down my cheeks as I told God I was miserable and confessed I had married for all the wrong reasons. I had tried everything that I knew to fix my brokenness and make my husband happy. I told God that my efforts hadn't worked. I couldn't do it. I prayed that if He would help me and teach me what I needed to know and to do, I promised that I would do whatever He wanted. I was at the end of myself.

"I ALWAYS TRY TO BE ATTENTIVE TO WHERE GOD HAS PLACED ME."

I arrived home to find a flyer in my front door. A neighbor in my cul-de-sac was throwing a block party that weekend and invited my husband and me to come. We went, and after we met this couple, they invited us to a neighborhood gathering for worship and Bible study in their home every Sunday evening—house church plant.

My husband was not interested, but I immediately remembered my promise and knew that God had heard my prayer. Before I even arrived home that day, He had heard me and heard the prayers of my neighbors. That felt so personal.

I spent the next six weeks studying the Bible and hearing the gospel in a way that I understood for the first time. I had no problem admitting I was a sinner. Accepting Jesus and what He accomplished for me on the cross was a gift of new life. After six weeks of studying the Bible I counted the cost, made my profession of faith, and was baptized by immersion in the center of that very cul-de-sac surrounded by neighbors, friends, and brothers and sisters in Christ. I still remember that joyous event!

Since then, I always try to be attentive to where God has placed me—my neighborhood. It is the center of real community for me and my prayer field. When I make myself available and open my home to gather, engage, listen, and serve, God shows me those who are reaching out and feeling their way for Him because He has been drawing them to Himself. My neighbors love and serve my family too. It is the economy of God.

The gospel is the power of God unto salvation. I get to pray, be in community, and share Jesus. Sometimes it's a neighborhood BBQ, a holiday event, Christmas caroling, a game night, or just having coffee or breakfast. Sometimes it's even a spontaneous invitation for a drink and conversation on my or a neighbor's front porch or back patio. Even better, it's a neighborhood Bible study. I have watched many of my neighbors hear the same invitation from Jesus to join His family and receive the gift of salvation.

It's an amazing feeling to wake up every morning almost thirty years later and still know that my sins are not counted against me. That's GOOD NEWS. Jesus did it all...I'm still following Him. My neighborhood is where I start.

A time for reflection

Gilbert K. Chesterton made the point very clear, "We make our friends; we make our enemies; but God makes our next-door neighbor."[4] We are living where we are for a reason, because God placed us there to be a light to those around us. Natalie experienced this firsthand, and now she has chosen to show that same kind of light to those where she lives.

In his book *Evangelism in the Early Church*, Michael Green pointed out that early leaders of the Church had an effective plan: "Christian missionaries made a deliberate point of gaining whatever households they could as lighthouses, so to speak, from which the gospel could illuminate the surrounding darkness."[5] He pointed out that the early Church stressed the centrality of the household for the advancement of Christianity. Is your home a lighthouse? What would it take for your home to emanate the kind of light that those in Natalie's neighborhood and those early Christians expressed?

Respond

Everyone is known for something in their neighborhood. What do you think you are known for by your neighbors? What are some things you could change to be known more as a person of hope?

_____

_____

_____

_____

Natalie Wright-Ruiz has been happily married—the second time around—for twenty-six years. She and her husband, Jim, have three adult children and one granddaughter. They live in the San Fernando Valley. Natalie is a spiritual director with her own private practice. She still spends a lot of time loving and being loved by her neighbors and following Jesus.

8

What's in a Name?

No longer will you be called Abram; your name will be Abraham. —Genesis 17:5

The man said, "Your name will no longer be Jacob, but Israel, because you have struggled with God and with humans and have overcome." —Genesis 32:28

Names are very important to God. He changed the names of certain people in the Bible to describe such things as destiny and character. He changed Abram's name, which means "high father," to Abraham, which means "father of a multitude." He changed Jacob's name, which means "trickster" or "usurper" to Israel, which means "he fights or persists with God." When Jesus looked at Simon, He said: "'You are Simon son of John. You will be called Cephas' (which, when translated, is Peter)" (John 1:42). Cephas is a common noun meaning "stone" or "rock."

Names are also very important to your neighbors. One of the first things you will want to learn is your neighbors' names. When you ask for a neighbor's name, you communicate that that person has significance. When you remember that neighbor's name and call him or her by name, you are on the doorstep of establishing a new relationship. Bruce beautifully portrays this very thing in his story.

Bruce and Karen Zachary's Neighborhood (A Condo)

"What's in a name? That which we call a rose by any other name would smell as sweet."[6]

Romeo Montague and Juliet Capulet meet and fall in love in Shakespeare's lyrical tale of "star-crossed lovers." They are doomed from the start as members of two warring families. In the quote just mentioned, Juliet tells Romeo that a name is an artificial and meaningless convention and that she loves the person who is called *Montague*, not the "Montague name," and not the Montague family.

Yet, names are significant. They convey meaning and imply relationship. Consider Jesus. His name tells us His mission: that Jehovah is "salvation." He is called Immanuel meaning "God with us." He is the Bread of Life; the Light of the World; the Door; the Good Shepherd; the Resurrection and the Life; the Way, the Truth, and the Life; and the True Vine.

Consider: Phyllis, Don and Tena, Jim and Marylee, Dave and Donna, Art and Rose, Ted and Diana, and Jeff and Sheri. Names that I would have been hard-pressed to recall a few years ago, but today flow to my memory with a fragrance more delightful than the most splendid of flowers. They are the names of my neighbors, people who live in close proximity to me and people who are my friends. People who I'm blessed to say I love.

Phyllis lives next door to Karen and me. We, along with our Neighborhood Group (small group Bible study), just celebrated her ninety-second birthday. She lives independently, has good health, and has a mind that remains remarkably sharp. Phyllis loves Jesus and says profound things that inspire the rest of the group. Last night, she reminded us that we might think that she is lonely, but she isn't because she knows that Jesus is with her. Karen has recently been sick, and Phyllis encouraged us to ask her should we need anything. These are precious words from a woman we love and who loves us, and we've been blessed to declare that truth together frequently.

"JESUS VALUES NEIGHBORS, AND THUS I'VE LEARNED THE IMPORTANCE OF LOVING MINE."

Don and Tena live on the other side of us. Don is a retired dentist, and Tena has retired from interior design. They both love Jesus and are very active in their service at a local church in our community. Don recently had a heart incident and was taken to the hospital in the middle of the night. The next day, I went to the hospital. As a pastor, hospital visits are part of the rhythm of my calling. However, this was the first time that I was motivated to do so for a neighbor as opposed to a congregant. I love that Don and Tena and Karen and I pray together. I love Don and Tena and know that I'm loved by them.

Jim and Marylee are a delight. They are fun and great to converse with and share a neighborhood with. They are hospitable, thoughtful, and caring, the kind of neighbors you'd ask to care for your pets while you're out of town and who would gladly do so.

They worship at the nearby Catholic parish church, and although we have significant doctrinal differences, I truly believe that they love Jesus. And we genuinely love and care for one another.

Dave and Donna live kitty-corner to us. Dave is the head of our homeowner's association (HOA). He had a recent back surgery with some complications. He's a stoic guy and has declined any offers of help. We told Donna to let us know if she needs any help. Dave serves our HOA faithfully, and I'm grateful for him. We've had lunch together, and I got to hear some of his story. He told me recently, "Bruce, you're a really good neighbor." Those were some of the most encouraging words that I've heard.

Art and Rose live directly across from us. They are very involved in a local church where they provide lay counseling assistance. Karen says that Rose has the complexion of a nineteen-year-old. She is a property manager, and she and Art own several properties. Art's first wife passed from consequences of dementia. Art has the wonderful gifts of irreverent (but never inappropriate) humor and great compassion. A rare blend. I love these two neighbors.

Ted and Diana are new to our neighborhood. They have an adult daughter with dystonia who requires an abundance of their energy and care. I admire their love for and attention to her. I often ask if there is anything Karen and I, or our other neighbors, can do to support them. I confess, I'm so inadequate to offer any help with their daughter's condition, but if bringing a meal or going to the store could help, I'd be glad to. I'm praying for their salvation, for strength, and for God's grace to be upon them. Ted grew up in a Jewish home, as did I, and if nothing else, he finds it amusing that his neighbor is a pastor with a mezuzah on the door.

Jeff and Sheri moved in less than a year ago and live across from us. Jeff is a pilot, and Sheri is an author. They both are really sharp, which I admire. I rarely see them outside; they probably are pretty busy with life. I hope to get to know them better this year. It was fun having them in our place for a recent HOA meeting and getting to talk with them and other neighbors.

Thus, there is so much in a name. Relationship, familiarity, and identity are connected to names. To Jesus' name is connected salvation, relationship, familiarity with God, and new identity. Jesus values neighbors, and thus I've learned the importance of loving mine. And in the process, my life is better. I'm more content, and I'm confident the love that I share with my neighbors honors God.

A time for reflection

What Bruce beautifully expressed about his relationship with his neighbors was not always the case. A little over two years ago after Bruce attended a neighboring conference, the Lord spoke to him and asked him, *So how many neighbors do you know?* It brought such conviction that he concluded that he was in rebellion to God and the Lord's greatest commandment. It has radically changed the course of his life with his neighbors and the direction of those in his congregation. So, the question is, How many neighbors do you know? Do you know their names? If you were to move tomorrow, would you be missed?

Respond

Knowing your neighbors' names is key in showing you care for them. Make a map of your neighborhood. Fill in the names you already know. Make it your mission to get to know all the names of your neighbors and fill out your map.

Bruce Zachary was raised in a Jewish home and came to faith in Christ as Messiah over twenty-five years ago. He was an attorney for twenty-five years. He and his wife, Karen, married in 1991 and have two sons, Joshua and Jonathan. Bruce taught at Calvary Chapel Costa Mesa's School of the Bible and is a graduate of CCCM's School of Ministry. In 1996 he planted Calvary Nexus in Camarillo, California, where he continues to serve as lead pastor. Bruce is the author of twelve books and serves as the director of the Calvary Church Planting Network, a global church planting initiative.

9

Instant Obedience to the Lord's Voice

The LORD came and stood there, calling as at the other times, "Samuel! Samuel!" Then Samuel said, "Speak, for your servant is listening." —1 Samuel 3:10.

Then I heard the voice of the Lord saying, "Whom shall I send? And who will go for us?" And I said, "Here am I. Send me!" —Isaiah 6:8

Samuel and Isaiah heard the Lord's voice and responded in obedience to His call. Throughout the Scriptures, the Lord called His people to do a variety of things. He called Moses to lead God's people out of slavery; He called Gideon to deliver the Israelites from the Midianites' oppression; He called Jonah to go to Nineveh and to preach against it; He called Mary to give birth to Jesus, the Son of God; and He called Peter to go to Cornelius's house to bring the gospel to the Gentiles. There are many more accounts like this. In some cases, obedience was immediate, and in other cases, it wasn't. The effect of instant obedience to God's voice is life-changing for us and for those we touch. It requires flexibility and a willingness to die to our plans and give way to His. Let's observe how Debi responded to the Lord's voice.

Debi Smith Wineroth's Neighborhood

For thirty-five years Mary lived next door to my dad and stepmother. Mary's children were grown and gone, spread out all over the state of Arizona. They found it hard to find time to visit her, so it just seemed natural to adopt her into our family. She spent many holidays and birthdays with us over the years. After my stepmother lost her battle with ovarian cancer and my father was alone, I found myself visiting her every time I went to see my dad. I would take her some dinner and we'd talk for a while. And sometimes I'd take over some popcorn and a movie. As time went by, she needed rides to and from the doctor's office, and I was happy to take her when my father couldn't. She had a serious asthmatic condition, and with age it just seemed to be getting worse. The doctor's visits were becoming a weekly routine, and she seemed to be growing much more frail.

"YOU NEED TO GO BACK AND SEE MARY TODAY."

I was a flight attendant, so I'd be gone three or four days at a time. During one of those times my father called and said that they had taken Mary away in an ambulance. After returning home I tracked down her son's phone number and called to ask where she was and how she was doing. He told me that her lungs had weakened so much that they'd put her into a hospice care facility. He said that the doctors had given her six months to live, and she had decided not to die at home. I told him I was leaving the next day for a four-day trip and that I'd see her when I returned home. I asked him to please pass on that message. "Don't worry," he said, "she'll be around for several more months; you'll have time."

Later that day my father and I were eating lunch, and we were planning to work in his garden when we finished. While enjoying my lunch and our conversation, I heard God whisper into my ear (as if He were sitting next to me), *You need to go back and see Mary today.* When I told my dad about my clear orders from the Lord, he said, "Well, we'll just have to work on the garden next week." So off I went to see Mary.

We were having a very pleasant visit when one of the staff came in and began a conversation. Apparently when Mary was admitted they talked about advance directives, and she had instructed them that if she stopped breathing, they were to attempt to revive her. Her son, however, had just called and stated that she had changed her mind and now wanted to be listed as a DNR (Do Not Resuscitate). She said "Yes, that is true. I don't want to live like this anymore. I wouldn't wish this on my worst enemy." The staff member said that they had written up new paperwork with new instructions and that they just needed a signature and a witness. She asked Mary if her "friend" could be the witness, and Mary said, "Yes, Debi is like a daughter to me." So, I signed the papers and we returned to our conversation.

About ten minutes later Mary began to struggle for air. I called for a nurse, and she put some liquid under Mary's tongue, but it didn't seem to help at all. Mary continued to struggle for every breath. I held her hand and looked from her to the nurse and back again, wondering why the nurse wasn't doing anything further to help her. And that's when it hit me! We had just signed a DNR!

They couldn't do anything further for her because she had just asked them not to. So, I continued to hold her hand as she took labored breaths and then stopped breathing. Mary knew the Lord, and it reflected on her face as she passed from this life into eternity with Him.

When all was said and done and I was walking out of that hospital in a daze, I asked, "Why, Lord? Why did You have me come today to witness this? This was painful!" But God spoke to me once again, and He said, *I called you here so that Mary wouldn't die alone.*

I wish that I could say I'm always obedient when I hear the Lord speak, but this time I was, and it meant so much to her family to know that their mother wasn't alone in her final moments.

A time for reflection

Does God speak to us today like He did to Debi? Her story certainly bears witness to the impeccable timing of the Lord for her to be by Mary's side as she slipped into eternity. Debi's sensitivity to God's voice allowed her to join her heavenly Father in Mary's homegoing. The Lord set it all up, and because of Debi's instant obedience she was in the right place at the right time. I admire how she and her father willingly adjusted their plans to God's greater plan (*kairos*). Think of what would have happened if she had not instantly obeyed the Lord's voice? How flexible are you when God has another plan for you in a day? Are you driven by *chronos*, your own plans and schedule? What would it take for you to be sensitive to the Lord's voice and instantly obey Him? Take some time to consider this with the Lord, so you will be available to the Lord when He calls on you.

Respond

In order to hear God speak to us, we need to spend time listening to God in prayer. What can you do to implement a regular time to listen to what God is telling you about your neighbors?

_____

_____

_____

_____

After thirty years as a flight attendant, Debi Smith Wineroth retired and moved from Phoenix, Arizona, to Chico, California, to become a full-time volunteer with Youth With A Mission (YWAM). She found her love for missions work while vacationing in Mexico. God had presented an opportunity for her to serve in the poorest communities, and while doing that she realized that she'd found her calling. In her retirement years, her traveling continues, but as a YWAMer she is "serving" in a totally different way.

10

Lessons from My Dog About Loving My Neighbor

Hearing that Jesus had silenced the Sadducees, the Pharisees got together. One of them, an expert in the law, tested him with this question: "Teacher, which is the greatest commandment in the Law?" Jesus replied: "'Love the Lord your God with all your heart and with all your soul and with all your mind.' This is the first and greatest commandment. And the second is like it: 'Love your neighbor as yourself.' All the Law and the Prophets hang on these two commandments." —Matthew 22:34–40

The teacher who asked Jesus which is the greatest commandment didn't expect Jesus' response because he intended to test Jesus. But Jesus pointed out that all the law and the prophets hang on these two commandments. Jesus' response silenced those who were trying to trap Him. His critics did not have a comeback. It is hard for us in the Church to imagine that everything we do boils down to these two commands. We often are looking for something new to do—a new strategy, a new method, a new program, or a new seminar covering the next life-changing anecdote. But Jesus clearly stated that these two commandments are it. We don't need to look any further. Once the eyes of a disciple of Jesus are open to this life-giving truth, he pursues it with all his heart because this is what Jesus gave His life to while He was here on earth. Sometimes we need a friend to help us understand this truth as Shah did in his story.

Shah and Karen Afshar's Neighborhood

I never wanted a dog. As my kids were growing up, they used to beg me to get them a pet. I always said no for two reasons. First, I knew that within a couple of days, I'd become the sole caregiver of said pet. But second, and even more importantly, I'd get so attached to the animal that its departure from this world would hurt me deeply. However, this all ended with my son's decision.

A few months before getting married, Todd decided to get a dog, which he couldn't keep after moving into his new home. So, by default, Karen and I became the proud owners of a six-month-old, highly active chocolate lab named Cocoa.

From day one, it was obvious that Cocoa was a people's dog. She disliked other dogs with a passion, but loved people with the same intensity. What she loved even more than people though, was chasing and fetching a little red KONG ball that we had to throw for her a good three to five times a day for at least ten to thirty minutes.

Once when I lost my job, our morning routine became crossing the street and me throwing the ball for Cocoa to fetch while I read a book. It was during this routine that I decided to wave at anyone who drove by. This was my first step toward getting to know my neighbors.

"I'VE HAD THE HONOR OF FULFILLING THE GREATEST COMMANDMENT CHRIST HAS GIVEN US."

It was sad and unfortunate that after living in my neighborhood for fourteen years, I knew very few of my neighbors. Cocoa changed that. Because of that simple act of waving at strangers, little by little I got to know everyone on my block. Some I got to know because they were happy to be recognized and respected by a simple wave or a nod. On several occasions, drivers pulled over just to say something like, "Sir, you've been waving at me for the last two years, so I thought it's about time I introduce myself to you." But others I got to know because they were intrigued by Cocoa's ability to fetch the ball.

In any case, because of Cocoa, in a couple of years, I achieved what I hadn't done in fourteen prior years—I got to know almost everyone on my block by name. All the neighbors and their children knew Cocoa by name even when they couldn't remember mine. They referred to me as Cocoa's dad. But there was more.

When the house across the street was sold to a new owner, my new neighbor put up a fence around the house. The new fence prevented Cocoa and me from continuing with our daily routine. So, we moved to the park half a mile away from our house. In the park, I used a plastic arm to catapult the famous red ball even farther and to encourage Cocoa to work even harder. But even more delightful for me was getting to meet more of my neighbors.

Even my wife, Karen, who only took Cocoa for a walk on weekends, has come to know many of the neighbors. It wasn't unusual for them to walk up to Karen, scream, "Cocoa," ask where I was, and introduce themselves to Karen.

In the last twelve years, Cocoa has seen me through a lot of pain. She saw me through cancer, the death of my dad and both my in-laws, our daughter's near-death car accident, the devastating experience of losing a job I loved, our children's hardships, and more. Through it all, her faithfulness has been impeccable. I pray I can be half as faithful to my loved ones as she's been to me.

Because of Cocoa, I've had the honor of fulfilling the greatest commandment Christ has given us—loving my neighbors as myself. I've had the privilege of sharing the gospel and praying with my neighbors in a very natural and simple way that started by me recognizing them as human beings who deserved to be waived at. But things have changed.

Over a month ago, Cocoa was diagnosed with heart and lung cancer. These days she doesn't chase her ball anymore. Almost every day, she lies on the front lawn (sometimes for ten to twelve hours) and sleeps. These days, my office is in our garage where I sit and watch my best friend, Cocoa, nearing her end while I still wave at all who drive by.

A time for reflection

Shah honestly and humbly shares how long it took him to begin to love his neighbors. I think many of us, if we were honest like Shah, would have to admit that we have overlooked being obedient to the Lord's greatest commandment. We might respond with, "I love God," but what about the second part of the great commandment? It is very moving that God used Cocoa to nudge Shah toward loving his actual neighbors, and it all started with waving to his neighbors.

Who or what is God using in your life to nudge you toward loving your actual neighbors? What would it take to begin to wave at your neighbors and even start up a conversation? Is the Lord speaking to you about this very thing? Remember the significance of instant obedience.

Respond

Shah's story is really just about being visible in your community. What is one way you can be more visible to your neighbors?

_____

_____

_____

_____

Shah Afshar founded and pastored the first Iranian-Christian organization in the United States. He has been instrumental in reaching the Muslim world with the gospel. His work as a professor and as a Muslim world mission coordinator for Foursquare Missions International has expanded his influence worldwide. As a former Muslim and seminary-trained leader, Shah shares unique insights with humor and wit. His passion is to communicate the relevance of Christ's message to a skeptical generation. Shah is available to speak at conventions, churches, schools, and for TV or radio interviews.

11

Bringing in God's Kingdom

[Jesus] told them another parable: "The kingdom of heaven is like a mustard seed, which a man took and planted in his field. Though it is the smallest of all seeds, yet when it grows, it is the largest of garden plants and becomes a tree, so that the birds come and perch in its branches." He told them still another parable: "The kingdom of heaven is like yeast that a woman took and mixed into about sixty pounds of flour until it worked all through the dough." —Matthew 13:31–33

We are so different from Jesus in the way we would like to see His kingdom grow. We think something big is needed, but Jesus says it starts small like a tiny mustard seed or a little bit of yeast in flour. Little by little it persistently grows and will take over and change the character of those in a neighborhood.

A lady once asked me at a seminar in Denver, "How can loving my neighbors have any impact on the city of Denver?" I responded to her question by referring to the Parable of the Mustard Seed and the Parable of the Yeast and the Flour; if she loved her neighbors, eventually the seed of her love would impact all of Denver. Now, that may sound like an overstatement, but Jesus knew that love of this nature is contagious. In time, others will begin to jump onboard, and before long you have a movement that has spread throughout a neighborhood and beyond. Let's observe how the seeds of love began to take over Charlene and Gary's neighborhood and spread to other neighborhoods as well.

Charlene and Gary Miller's Neighborhood

As director of Neighborhood Watch for fifteen years with the Boise City Police Department in Boise, Idaho, I was tasked with promoting safe neighborhoods. In the beginning, I taught residents that neighbors working together can reduce and prevent certain types of crime. In response to criminal activity, someone would want to start a Neighborhood Watch group, contacting me to help them initiate a group because they had been victimized. I would meet with and speak to residents about crime prevention, offering measures they could implement, and encouraging them to watch out for each other and their property. Crime would be reduced due to their diligence.

I soon realized that after crime is reduced, which is the case when residents are watchful and take proper precautions, the diligence of some in the Neighborhood Watch program would decrease over time. That is, the passion and fervency which motivated them to act in the first place dwindled as effectiveness increased.

Of the over three hundred groups I helped coordinate, approximately 150 continued to thrive. I was interested in finding out what they did differently than those groups that started out strong and then lost interest. I interviewed many of the leaders and discovered it was the relationships they built with neighbors that were key to keeping neighborhoods safe, connected, and vibrant. They had block parties, talked to each other frequently, shared their garden produce, helped each other when someone was sick, and watched over a house while the owner was away on vacation. It was much more than passing on useful information. They came together in their neighborhood and took ownership of it because of the relationships they had cultivated.

My focus in the Neighborhood Watch program changed. I still wanted to assist them in reducing and preventing crime, and to use the practical measures I taught for that purpose. Yet to have a thriving neighborhood, our program encouraged the relationship aspect between neighbors even more than before. In these active groups where strong relationships were built between neighbors, crime rarely occurred.

Some of the group leaders were Christians. They shared with me that they regularly walked through their neighborhoods silently praying for the residents in each house. They were convinced it made a difference.

"THAT'S JUST WHAT WE DO IN THIS NEIGHBORHOOD."

My husband, Gary, and I live in a cul-de-sac of five houses. Three, including us, have lived next to each other for more than twenty-four years. Not all go to church or are even Christians, and they are not all of the same political persuasions or faith. Our involvement in each other's lives has grown over time. We have seen babies born and grandkids arrive, and together have experienced difficulties, sickness, retirement, and deaths. We have shared vegetables from our gardens, watched each other's houses when on vacation, fed each other's animals, shoveled snow, exchanged food and Christmas goodies, held a women's brunch and neighborhood BBQ, visited a neighbor in the hospital, and prayed for and with neighbors.

Recently a new neighbor, an older widow, was out on her front porch with her dog. We walked over to say hello, and neighbors from other houses came over to join us. We all talked with each other for a while. This is not uncommon. We are also friends with some residents beyond the cul-de-sac and are all on a first-name basis.

Our new elderly neighbor recently asked our next-door neighbor (who is not a Christian) why she fed our cat and watched our house while we were away for two weeks, wondering if we weren't somehow taking advantage of her. Our neighbor answered, "That's just what we do in this neighborhood. We take care of each other." Gary has gone over to her house more than once in the middle of the night to help pick her disabled husband up off the floor. This new neighbor has since brought brownies to us and others in the cul-de-sac, saying she was glad she moved here.

It hasn't always been this way. Neighbors have come and gone. One reclusive neighbor was uncomfortable with our attempts at friendliness, interpreting it as some sort of tit-for-tat manipulation. For example, if we did something for this neighbor, the person felt it meant an obligation to do something for us.

A few years ago, we read Lynn Cory's book *Neighborhood Initiative and the Love of God*. It rang true for us, especially since we had seen similar principles at work during our law enforcement careers. We were already friends with some of our neighbors, but we began to pray anew and ask God how we could better love our neighbors. We have seen this neighborly approach slowly grow and produce more fruit, like the mustard plant Jesus spoke of in Matthew 13.

We have made the choice, with God's help, to love our neighbors into His kingdom, leaving their hearts in His hands, expecting Jesus to work. He gives us *kairos* moments as we simply make ourselves available for His purposes. God is continuing to answer our prayer, and we are sure there's more to come.

A time for reflection

Charlene points out in her story that caring relationships, particularly on the part of Christians in a neighborhood, reduces crime and provides a safe place for people to live. We can learn a couple of things from Charlene's story. Building a caring community doesn't happen overnight. It takes time to build this kind of relationship among neighbors. It also necessitates being available to your neighbors when there is a need.

Once, an elderly woman who was a part of a small group in our home, said to me, "I know what you are up to—you are up to 24/7." She went on to explain, saying, "We can go on a short-term mission's trip to Mexico, but when the trip is over, we come back to our normal lives. But loving our neighbors requires 24/7." She was right, although this is not what I am up to. This is what the Great Commandment, loving God and loving our neighbors, is all about. This is how Jesus lived His life when He lived among us.

Respond

What words would you use to describe your neighborhood? If your neighborhood lacks community, what would it take to begin to foster relationships among your neighbors?

_____

_____

_____

_____

_____

Charlene and Gary Miller both recently retired from law enforcement careers. Gary was a deputy sheriff, working as a patrol officer and a training officer for Ada County, Idaho. Charlene was a member of the crime prevention unit with Boise City Police, responsible for Neighborhood Watch programs and teaching personal safety and crime prevention on local, state, and national levels. They have also been volunteer pastors of an adult singles group, counseled married couples, and led Bible studies. Married for forty years, they have three children and seven grandchildren. They have known Lynn and jo Cory since the 1970s.

12

Doing What the Father Is Doing

My Father is always at his work to this very day, and I too am working.... Very truly I tell you, the Son can do nothing by himself; he can do only what he sees his Father doing, because whatever the Father does the Son also does. For the Father loves the Son and shows him all he does. Yes, and he will show him even greater works than these, so that you will be amazed.
—John 5:17, 19–20

If Jesus could do nothing by Himself, then certainly we must become equally dependent, joining with the Father where He is already at work, if we truly want to see something happen with our neighbors.

Our Lord lived out His earthly ministry as His Father presented Him with one divine opportunity after another. Jesus wasn't out to make things happen; instead, He joined with His Father in what He was doing. The activities of Jesus' life were driven by His relationship with His Father, His sensitivity to the Spirit, and His loving service to the people around Him. This is *kairos* and such a freeing way to begin to love your neighbors. This story by Lin beautifully exhibits how the Father worked to engage him with his neighbors.

Lin and Daryl Franklin's Neighborhood

My wife and I were thinking about attending Together 2016, a Christian revival gathering on the National Mall in Washington, D.C. But, it was a long way to travel for a one-day event, so we put the decision on hold. A few weeks later, we discovered that an evangelism conference was scheduled in DC the day beforehand, so we decided to make the six-hour drive and attend both the revival and the conference. And that's where we met Lynn Cory.

The conference room layout was a bunch of round tables for discussion, and Lynn was at our table. He had a chance to share with our table about his ministry, and I was intrigued. I thought about how the concept is so simple—our most natural opportunity for evangelism is right in front of us, our neighbors. And I realized that even though we live in a neighborhood that is perfect for frequent contact with our neighbors, we didn't really know any of them. Lynn gave us a copy of his book, *Neighborhood Initiative and the Love of God*, before we left.

"THIS IS GOD'S RODEO, NOT MINE; I WILL JUST BE OBEDIENT."

We returned from Washington, and I got busy again and forgot all about the revelation I had that day. But God hadn't! A few months later He suddenly put it on my heart to find the book Lynn gave me and to read it. I did. And I knew God didn't nudge me to read the book just for enjoyment He wanted me to take action, to implement the suggestions in the book. So, for the next few months I began praying for opportunities to meet our neighbors and prayer-walked the neighborhood a bit. Probably just as important, I actually made an effort for the first time to look for opportunities to meet them.

Over several months God arranged some divine meetings. The first was during the winter. I had finally finished snow-blowing my driveway and sidewalk, and I put the snow blower away in the garage and started walking back to my front door, exhausted. And God put this thought in my mind: *How about the neighbor's sidewalk?* I kept walking until I suddenly realized that this could be an answer to my neighborhood prayer walks. So, I walked back to the garage, started the snowblower, and did the sidewalk in front of our next-door neighbor's house. And I was thinking, *What a waste of time. Sure, it's a nice thing to do, but I don't think our neighbor is even home.* But as I reached the end of his sidewalk, I ran into the neighbor two houses over and asked if he wanted me to do his sidewalk too. He said he had a snow blower, but it wasn't working. So I did his sidewalk too and we got a chance to meet and chat.

A month or so later, my wife and I were walking down our street and saw a husband and wife trying to lift some heavy furniture out of a truck and into their house. We asked if they wanted help, and the wife eagerly accepted. It was a difficult task, with one piece needing to go up a tight stairwell, but we persevered. The wife whispered as we left, "I think you just saved my marriage." I was really excited that God was showing up, but I had still only met a few neighbors.

A young couple with a baby had recently moved in, and for some reason my attention was drawn to that house. But nothing happened! These people were like ghosts—I never saw them. But one day as I drove into our driveway and looked over at their house, there she was getting out of the car with her baby. I almost sprinted over to meet her, and we had a nice conversation.

And only a few days later, God suddenly said to me, *When are you going to have the party?* He knew I had been thinking about inviting the neighbors over at some point so we could all connect with each other. In my head, I came up with an excuse, which was true—the timing was not ideal since we had a lot going on. And God said, *How about the Saturday ten days from now* And I thought, *Well yes, that date is open, but it's too close. We need to get invitations, send them, and give time for responses. Even if we do all this, no one will come anyway on such short notice.* God repeated, *How about the Saturday ten days from now* And I thought, *This is God's rodeo, not mine; I will just be obedient.*

I went out the next day, bought the invitations, and sent them out, inviting everyone to a two-hour snacks and drinks get-together in our backyard from 4:00 to 6:00 p.m. I invited six couples and their families, put the invitations in each of their mailboxes, and waited for the email RSVPs. And guess what? All but one couple responded, and all the responses were yes! And the weather the day of the party was perfect! We had fourteen adults and nine of their kids. And yes, the couple that didn't RSVP also showed up, so God arranged 100 percent attendance. It was a great time of getting to know one another, and we even were invited to one neighbor's Christmas party.

I thought, *Wow, this all started many months ago with a conference we never really wanted to attend, and look where God has led us.* It's not clear exactly where He'll lead from here, but it's clear that God is using us to help bring the neighborhood together, and we look forward to His next nudge.

A time for reflection

Lin's story allows us to listen in on a dialogue between him and the Father. So often the Lord is speaking to us, like He did to Lin, and we write it off as our own thoughts. Yet the Lord truly communicates with us today and will direct us to do something with a neighbor or even to put on an event like Lin did. You know how when you notice something for the first time, like how many black, white, or gray cars there are on the road, that you can't stop noticing it everywhere you go? When it's on our radar, we are in tune, we are in *kairos* time.

Did you see how Lin was praying and then "made an effort for the first time to look for opportunities to meet them"? This shouldn't be overlooked. Habakkuk 2:1 says "I will stand at my watch and station myself on the ramparts; I will look to see what he will say to me." Lin prayed and looked to see how God was moving. We may find ourselves hearing the Lord's voice, but then we just don't want to do what He is asking us to do. It may be too threatening. I have found if we stay in our comfort zone, we miss out on experiencing the best life. Faith is spelled R-I-S-K.

When you begin to respond to God's voice in obedience, you are tuned in to hear Him more clearly and more often. Begin to ask the Lord to speak to you about your neighbors and what He would like you to do. Has He already been speaking to you about a neighbor or asking you to initiate an event in your neighborhood? What is He asking you to do? Are you now willing to join Him in His work?

Respond

What is something that you have felt in your heart when it comes to your neighborhood, but you have not acted on it because it feels like too much of a risk?

_____

_____

_____

_____

Lin Franklin is a retired businessman. He lives with his wife, Daryl, in Darien, Connecticut, and they are enjoying their new role as grandparents. God has opened up many different opportunities for them to join Him in His plans. What a great ride it has been!

13

Look for People of Peace

When you enter a house, first say, "Peace to this house." If someone who promotes peace is there, your peace will rest on them; if not, it will return to you. Stay there, eating and drinking whatever they give you, for the worker deserves his wages. Do not move around from house to house. When you enter a town and are welcomed, eat what is offered to you. Heal the sick who are there and tell them, "The kingdom of God has come near to you." But when you enter a town and are not welcomed, go into its streets and say, "Even the dust of your town we wipe from our feet as a warning to you. Yet be sure of this: The kingdom of God has come near." —Luke 10:5–11

When Jesus sent out the seventy disciples, He directed them to go into communities and look for those in neighborhoods who would welcome them, literally, into their homes. But in addition to the disciples being received, this welcoming spirit also meant that those in the home would receive the disciple's teaching. Jesus clarified this when He told His disciples, "Whoever listens to you, listens to me; whoever rejects you rejects me; but whoever rejects me rejects him who sent me" (Luke 10:16).

Understanding what Jesus is saying here is freeing for us today as we work to spread the gospel. So often we feel the burden is on us to make people like us and to arm-twist them into receiving the gospel message, when the exact opposite is true. Jesus put the responsibility on the recipient to become a seeker of truth.

It is up to the recipients to welcome you. They may be attracted to something in you (Jesus) and desire what you have. Perhaps they have been thinking about spiritual things for some time and will be drawn to you without knowing why. They may say something like, "You have a peace about you," or, "I like your family. You seem so different." They might even say, "I like you," or, "I like being with you." Whatever it is, they will take a liking to you. These are signs of a welcoming person or a person of peace.

The term "person of peace" implies that the person's heart has been prepared and is open to Jesus and the gospel. He or she is someone to whom God has been speaking and who He has been preparing to meet up with one of His children.

A person who receives God's peace has had an encounter, or rather, a lifetime of encounters, that prepares him or her for salvation and discipleship. God's peace rests on that person because God's favor is with him or her; as it says in Luke 2:14, "On earth peace to those on whom his favor rests." Jesus instructed His disciples, "When you enter a house, first say, 'Peace to this house.' If someone who promotes peace is there, your peace will rest on them; if not, it will return to you" (Luke 10:5–6). The following story is a perfect example of a person of peace, one whose heart was prepared by God to receive the life-changing gospel.

Lynn and Jo Cory's Neighborhood (Apartment)

When Jo and I were first married, we lived in an apartment complex. We intentionally got to know our neighbors and looked out for them. It was a friendly environment where everyone knew each other's names and stopped to talk with one another. Our building had a good mix of older and younger people. One of those neighbors, Don, took a liking to me. I was in my mid-twenties and he was sixty, which I thought was really old. We talked often. His wife, Connie, was the life of the apartment building. She was always out by the pool working on her year-round tan. Connie was loud with a fun sense of humor and was loved by everyone.

"I HAVE BEEN WATCHING YOUR LIFE, AND I WANT WHAT YOU HAVE."

One day, I invited Don to church, and much to my surprise, he began to attend regularly. Once, at the back of our little chapel, he said to me, "I have been watching your life, and I want what you have." I was quite surprised that a man of his age would humble himself to a man in his twenties. After I shared a short explanation of the gospel, Don made a commitment to Christ.

Not long after this, Don asked if my pastor and I could come over and pray for Connie, who was Jewish. She had been diagnosed with terminal cancer, and the doctors did not give her long to live. She could not even get out of bed on her own. My pastor and I joined Don in his apartment's living room to pray for Connie. When we finished praying, she came bounding out of her bedroom joyfully yelling, "You did this to me! You did this to me!" And then she started doing jumping jacks in front of us. We were amazed! My pastor shared the gospel with her, and she invited the Lord into her life.

A week later Connie slipped away into the Lord's presence. Don asked if I would conduct a small memorial service for her in their apartment. We had a sweet gathering, and many people in the apartment building joined us to celebrate Connie's life. She had added so much life and laughter to our little community, and her presence was deeply missed.

A time for reflection

Don and Connie's story had years of history prior to their meeting jo and me. These were years in which God was beautifully at work preparing their hearts for the gospel message. I don't believe my life alone brought Don to a point of being ready for the gospel. However, this story reminds me that I am an integral part of the Great Commission, a part of joining in the work others began. In this case, I was privileged enough to see the fruition of God's work in Don and Connie's lives.

We can't make these kinds of things happen, but we can join our Father in the work that He is doing in our neighbors' lives. Jesus sent out His disciples nearly two thousand years ago to start spreading the message of the gospel. At the time, there were not that many to carry the gospel forward. As Jesus said to His disciples, "The harvest is plentiful, but the workers are few" (Luke 10:2). Today, we, His disciples, are spread all over the world and have an opportunity to carry on this good work in the neighborhoods where He has placed us. It starts with the Lord's directive to look for people of peace, those who welcome you in your neighborhood, and then your blessing to them can follow.

Respond

Who in your neighborhood would you consider to be people of peace? Make a list of these people and begin to pray that the Lord opens a door for you to have a conversation with them about Jesus. Remember what Jesus said: "The one who hears you hears me" (Luke 10:16, ESV).

_____

_____

_____

_____

_____

_____

14

The Power of Love

> Listen, my dear brothers and sisters: Has not God chosen those who are poor in the eyes of the world to be rich in faith and to inherit the kingdom he promised those who love him?...If you really keep the royal law found in Scripture, "Love your neighbor as yourself," you are doing right. —James 2:5, 8

Loving our neighbor is one of the most powerful weapons in our arsenal as we fight against the darkness that permeates our world and the lives of those around us. Neighbors may be critical of us because we are Christians; however, once they experience the flow of God's love through us, they often find this attitude difficult to maintain. Jesus told us, "Let your light shine before others, that they may see your good deeds and glorify your Father in heaven" (Matthew 5:16). The word Jesus used here for "good" is *kalos*, which means "beautiful"...beautiful because the deeds glorify our heavenly Father. When we allow the light of God's love to be expressed toward our neighbors, they often find it attractive and are irresistibly drawn to it. This is true even in the case of desperate neighborhoods like Joe and Heidi's. Observe how God's love expressed through Joe's life impacted a young man named Danny.

Joe and Heidi White's Neighborhood (Jackson Neighborhood)

When I saw Danny for the first time, I knew he would cause us trouble. Danny was not just a typical teenager in our neighborhood; he was a known gang member. He wore the color red to indicate his gang, and he wore a scowl on his face. He wouldn't look you in the eyes when you said hello, and he would never dare to smile or even acknowledge you if you said hi. It was clear that he had a hard life, but it was also clear that he had a hard heart.

Occasionally, my wife and I saw Danny walking through the neighborhood, and we always made it a point to roll down our windows and yell, "Heeeeey, Daaaaaaany," and wave as we drove by. For months, he didn't even acknowledge us. The only reason we knew his name was because one evening he walked by our home and we asked him. He was apprehensive to tell us, undoubtedly uncertain as to why we'd even care to know.

What would it take to love Danny and others like him? Our neighborhood is filled with "Dannys." They hate school, have dysfunctional homes, are gang affiliated, and, in many cases, have criminal records. The "Dannys" in our neighborhood end up in one of three places: an early grave, jail, or a world of perpetual poverty. Along the way, they have extreme barriers to employment.

According to the latest Barna research (a visionary research and resource company), Fresno has the highest church attendance rate on the West Coast,[7] but it also has the second highest rate of concentrated poverty in the nation.[8] What does this mean? It means, at minimum, that church attendance isn't transforming our city's most desperate neighborhoods, and kids like Danny are becoming the latest statistics for crime rates and school dropout.

What does it mean that Jesus asked His Church to love their neighbor Danny? As a church in the Jackson Neighborhood, we obsessed about this question. He wouldn't come to church with us, and we couldn't force him to learn something at a school he hated. Under these desperate conditions, and with an obsession to love our neighbor Danny, an idea was born.

"THANKS FOR LOVING ME."

Behind our one-hundred year-old home sat an abandoned workshop that at one time was used as a mechanic's garage for the Jackson Neighborhood. It had been in a state of disrepair for the past one hundred years. We wondered if we could turn that workshop into an artisan space where neighborhood kids could learn job-transferable skills like welding and woodworking. Would kids like Danny, who have extreme barriers to employment, thrive in an environment outside of the classroom and in a scenario where learning was possible under the mentorship of skilled artisans?

For the next year, in an attempt to love our neighbor Danny, we renovated this shop into a beautiful space filled with high-end woodworking equipment. We created a business called Neighborhood Jobs, which would train and employ Danny to make Little Free Libraries. These little libraries are miniature houses that people mount on a post and often paint to match their home. They are filled with books that neighbors can take, donate, and return. They are a "little library" for your neighborhood.

One day, we invited Danny to come over to show him the workshop. He was amazed at all the cool woodworking equipment. We asked, "Danny, would you like to make money? We want to start a business that you would run. We will teach you how to make little libraries, and we will find effective ways to sell them. When we sell them, all the profit will go to you." To our surprise he said, "Yes!" Over the next year we taught Danny how to do just that. Hiring Danny to build Little Free Libraries provided an opportunity for him to prove his potential.

Danny used high-quality cedar, birch, and poplar, and all of his libraries were waterproof and durable. People bought them like crazy, and as sales increased so did his confidence. He began to smile and say hello. He began to exchange his gang colors for shirts that had the company logo. As his skills increased, so did his joy—he wasn't just a school dropout, he was a craftsman and a business owner. In the following year, he began to attend church with us in the neighborhood—each week he gathered with neighbors and participated in the community of neighbors.

Recently I asked him, "Danny, you've come a long way in these last few years. Do you see how much has changed in your life since we first met?" Danny isn't a "talker"; he's still quiet and reserved, but his response spoke volumes. He said, "Yeah." And after a long pause he said, "I'm gonna do something great with my life. Thanks for loving me."

Jesus, the Master Carpenter, is welcoming his apprentice Danny into a new future filled with hope and opportunity. Everything is possible when we love our neighbors.

A time for reflection

As you reflect on Danny's story, think of Joe's level of commitment to love him as himself. Who sacrifices like this for another person today? It is otherworldly. Back in the early '70s a little book by

Francis Schaeffer titled *The Mark of the Christian* had great influence in the body of Christ. The mark Schaeffer referred to is love, the love of God flowing through us to another human being. This is the kind of love that Joe demonstrated in Danny's life. The fact that Danny said, "Thanks for loving me," reveals that God's love touched his life in a profound way. Is the Lord calling you to love someone, particularly in your neighborhood? Who might that be? Are you ready to uncap the Lord's love and let it flow through you to this person? Where can you start? Ask the Lord to give you direction and then follow His lead.

Respond

How does this story challenge you to step out of your comfort zone?

_____

_____

_____

Joe White and his wife, Heidi, are the founders and lead pastors of Neighborhood Church in Fresno, California. He also runs a small business that employs people with barriers to employment and a nonprofit that meets specialized needs in their neighborhood with specific care. He has a bachelor of arts in biblical studies, a diploma in urban ministry, a diploma in Christian studies, and a master of divinity. Like all the Neighborhood Church staff, he lives in the Jackson Neighborhood with his wife and four kids. They absolutely adore their neighbors and neighborhood. Connect with them at www.joeandheidiwhite. blogspot.com or www.neighborhoodchurchfresno.com.

15

Will You Be My Neighbor?

Do not forsake your friend or a friend of your family, and do not go to your relative's house when disaster strikes you—better a neighbor nearby than a relative far away.
—Proverbs 27:10

This is one of the "Thirty Sayings of the Wise" in Proverbs. It emphasizes the importance of remaining in faithful relationship with friends and family, but then it says something that seems counterintuitive: don't go to a relative's house. You might ask, "Why not go to your relative's house when disaster strikes?" The saying makes perfect sense when people go through a disaster like an earthquake.

I lived through the 1994 Northridge earthquake, and after the earthquake, walls came down (literally too) between neighbors. Neighbors were helping neighbors in ways that you can't imagine, but after a time we all retreated to our old patterns. There is something to be said about geographic proximity when it comes to disasters. We hear it over and over again on the news, how the neighbors tenderly hold each other up following the all-too-familiar mass shootings, but should we only be there for our neighbors when tragedies occur? Mary Alice told me the following story about an elderly neighbor from her apartment complex that reveals what real commitment is like when it comes to loving your neighbor as yourself.

Mary Alice Pollok's Neighborhood

Jacob, my eighty-year-old neighbor, is Jewish. When his wife passed away from cancer two years ago, he fell into a deep depression. I contacted the other neighbors that he and I knew, and for almost a year we took turns delivering dinners to him and checking on him. When his spirits would sink low, my kids and I would drag him out of his apartment and take him to the pool. One night, however, he fell into a serious depression and tried to kill himself with some pills. I called 911 and stayed with him until the paramedics got there. They took him to the hospital and saved his life.

Afterward, he asked me why I cared so much about him when his own children did not even bother to keep in touch. I said the love and compassion I have for people comes from Jesus Christ. Jesus is who my neighbor has seen in action over the last year and a half. This opened up many more conversations about life and death. With the Jewish faith there is no hope—but with Jesus, He is our hope. My neighbor and I ran into each other weekly, and he gave me updates on his progress.

One night, I was deep in conversation with my fourteen-year-old son. Because I treasure and protect these times with my son, especially as he grows into a young man, I was screening my calls. That night my caller ID revealed it was Jacob.

"I'M JUST A NEIGHBOR."

Jacob had been calling our home regularly and never seemed to get back on his feet—regular phone calls, evening visits with homemade dinners four to five times a week, and weekend walks didn't seem to relieve his needs. In Jacob's own words, he was "a crotchety old Jewish man who doesn't make friends easily."

What a sight we had become in our community when we took our walks, a mother of two eighth graders happily chatting with a grumpy, disheveled old man. No one could figure that one out. But God had plans for this friendship.

When I answered the phone to see what Jacob needed, I heard breathing, but Jacob didn't respond to my questions. I threw on my warm coat, told my son not to worry, and bounded down three flights of stairs and over to the next building where Jacob lived.

As I approached his home, I found the front door ajar. I walked in and saw Jacob on the floor at the bottom of the stairs. He was clutching his chest and having difficulty breathing. I realized in a split second this was not one of his anxiety attacks. I called 911 and heard sirens responding almost immediately from the fire station up the hill. The paramedics arrived and began to do their work. A paramedic asked if he could speak with me. It took a great deal of effort to disentangle my hand from Jacob's since he was clutching it so tightly. His eyes filled with fear as he said, "Please don't leave me." I assured him I wouldn't. The paramedic asked me if I could provide medical information on "my father." I told him what I knew about Jacob's mental and physical condition and then explained I wasn't Jacob's daughter. "Then who are you?" he asked. I told him I was just a neighbor.

I followed the ambulance in my car and could see the terror on Jacob's face as medical personnel lifted him onto a hospital gurney. I asked the emergency room receptionist if I could see Jacob. The receptionist asked if I was a relative, but I said I was just a neighbor.

"You're kidding," the receptionist said, but he allowed me to go back in the triage area to see Jacob.

I held Jacob's hand as technicians drew blood and placed EKG patches on his chest. The nurse asked me privately how long my father had been in this deteriorated condition. I told her what I knew and ended the conversation (yet again) with, "He's not my father; I'm just a neighbor."

Shortly after medical staff wheeled Jacob into another room for further testing, the attending physician thanked me for keeping Jacob calm and asked the question I already knew was coming: "How are you related to Jacob?"

I responded, "I'm not related; I'm just a neighbor."

"I wish I had a neighbor like you," the doctor said.

As I left the emergency room, the doctor asked me with a giggle laced in seriousness, "Will you be my neighbor?"

A time for reflection

Like the attending physician Mary Alice met, I think we all would like to have a neighbor like her. More importantly, her heart is what our neighbors need from us, whether or not they realize it. In each case, when the hospital staff asked her if she was a relative and found out that she was just a neighbor, they shook their heads in amazement. Sadly, we live in a day when finding a good neighbor is a rarity. It's no wonder we see so much depression and so many people hurting each other with words on social media or at the extreme, with violence.

Good neighbors are few and far between. Our connectedness with one another could save countless lives. If Mary Alice had not adopted her neighbor as her own, what do you think would have happened to him? Wouldn't it be wonderful if the Church stepped up to become the good neighbor? I think that's the silent appeal of neighborhoods today. Will we respond?

Respond

Make a list of any older neighbors in your neighborhood. Pray about asking them if they have any relatives nearby in case of emergencies. Give them a card with your name and number on it in case they need some help in an emergency.

_____

_____

_____

_____

Mary Alice Pollok is a director of social services for a large hospice and palliative care company in Orange County, California. She holds a master's degree in ministry and a master's degree in social work, serves as an adjunct field professor for the University of Southern California, and is a consultant for the Veterans Affairs Hospital in Long Beach, California, serving female veterans with post-traumatic stress disorder. Mary Alice volunteers as a camp coordinator for children with terminal illness. Best of all, she is the proud mother of a son, Daniel, and daughter, Michelle.

16

Small Acts of Love Yield Great Return

In Joppa there was a disciple named Tabitha (in Greek her name is Dorcas); she was always doing good and helping the poor. About that time she became sick and died, and her body was washed and placed in an upstairs room. Lydda was near Joppa; so when the disciples heard that Peter was in Lydda, they sent two men to him and urged him, "Please come at once!" Peter went with them, and when he arrived he was taken upstairs to the room. All the widows stood around him, crying and showing him the robes and other clothing that Dorcas had made while she was still with them. Peter sent them all out of the room; then he got down on his knees and prayed. Turning toward the dead woman, he said, "Tabitha, get up." She opened her eyes, and seeing Peter she sat up. He took her by the hand and helped her to her feet. Then he called for the believers, especially the widows, and presented her to them alive. This became known all over Joppa, and many people believed in the Lord.
—Acts 9:36–42

When I read Susan's story, which follows, I was reminded of this story of Tabitha. Susan's faithfulness in loving her neighbors is not very significant by the world's standards, but just like Tabitha, she is clearly a disciple of Christ. Tabitha was one of only a handful of people to be raised from the dead in Scripture. There was something noteworthy about her, and here's what we can gather. We know Tabitha made garments, did good, and helped the poor. Tabitha in Hebrew means "beauty" and "grace." Could it be that the grace and goodness she embodied set the stage for the miraculous move of God resurrecting her? Take a look at Susan's gracious acts in her story and see if you can see God preparing the way for Him to move.

Susan Hanson's Neighborhood (Mobile Home Park)

After living in my condo for twenty-four years, I was moving to a senior mobile home park. A new season of my life was about to begin.

During the previous several years, while I lived at the condo, the Lord and I had become close friends. He pursued me, and I pursued Him. I meditated on His Word. I learned to listen to the Holy Spirit speak to me through His Word and to hear His still, small voice in prayer. I learned to watch and to listen for direction from Him and to obey. Looking back, I can see that His purpose was to mature me and to prepare me to serve Him.

Prior to my move, I felt certain that the mobile home park was going to be a mission field, a place for me to spread the love of God to my neighbors. I gladly accepted the "assignment," as I like to call it. Although I had no idea how I was to accomplish the assignment, I knew that God would show me in His timing.

"I PRAYED, 'OKAY, LORD WHAT'S NEXT?'"

I received a confirmation of the assignment shortly after I moved in. The Lord prompted me to turn on the radio at the perfect time to hear Lynn Cory in an interview regarding his book, *Neighborhood Initiative and the Love of God*. After reading the book, I had a short telephone conversation with Lynn. But I still needed specific direction as to how the Lord wanted me to show His love. I spoke with a couple of other Christians in the mobile home park. However, no one seemed to be interested in further sharing or ministering with me. The Lord did not appear to be opening doors or giving me direction. Nevertheless, I continued to pray and seek His will.

About four months later, I was inspired to bake mini pumpkin bread muffins for my neighbors and put them in little bags complete with a "Happy Thanksgiving" greeting. I personally hand-delivered one to each of the twenty neighbors on my street while introducing myself as their new neighbor. I was well received.

I prayed, "Okay, Lord, what's next?" I was directed to purchase secular Christmas cards, which I found at a dollar store, for the 160 homes in the mobile home park. At the Lord's prompting, I inserted a small card on which I wrote a note that said, "Hello. I am a new neighbor. I have some good news!" Then I wrote out John 3:16 and hand-delivered one to each home. Although I was uneasy and fearful, I followed the Lord's guidance to introduce myself. Unfortunately, my new neighbors did not respond.

That was three years ago. My latest assignment from the Lord is to give each of the residents a handmade birthday card as well as handmade Thanksgiving, Christmas, Valentine's Day, Easter, and Fourth of July cards. Even though the task seems overwhelming, past experiences proved He was faithful and would supply all my needs to accomplish what He asked me to do!

What I find interesting and really fun is to see how the Lord has "gifted" me for the assignment. I am neither a craft person nor an artist. Nor am I one to come up with new and unique ideas for the cards. I depend on Him to give me an idea of what the card is to look like and what He wants the message to express. He also directs me where to buy the supplies. On the blank side of a 3x5 index card I do some "whimsical" artwork. On the lined side, I write a message that the Lord gives me. I pray and wait for His lead.

Here is how one birthday card came about: At the beginning of December, I prayerfully asked the Lord for a birthday card idea. A few days later, at about 5:00 a.m., I heard the word *cheerleader*. *Oh, thank You, Lord!* Later that morning I searched Google for a simple cheerleader graphic and found a cheerleader jumping in the air. I drew a prototype and made a stencil. I embellished her pom-poms with colored tissue paper that coordinated with the colors in her outfit. I wrote "HIP-HIP HOORAY! It's _____ birthday!" On the back was a handwritten blessing: "May the Lord bless and keep you; May the Lord smile on you and be gracious to you; May the Lord show you His favor and give you His peace" (Numbers 6:24–26).

I go through a similar process with the Thanksgiving, Christmas, Valentine's Day, Easter, and Fourth of July cards. When, at times, I feel hesitant to convey a message that the Lord gives me for some holiday cards, I keep reassuring myself that the message is His (not something I made up), and that it is His ministry and His message. He knows what He wants to say to my neighbors and what they need to hear. I don't want to get in His way. I want to be obedient. I find peace in these truths.

The mobile home park residents look forward to receiving the cards. Many have told me that they keep them all. Some of the feedback I have received includes that they "feel loved," that the cards brighten their day, put a smile on their face, and makes them look to God, and they feel I am making the world a better place with the kindness contained in them. One recipient shared that "the cards were sources of comfort in the midst of a family crisis; the messages encouraged and helped them through it." Yet another respondent thanked me by saying, "The cards seem to come on a day when I really need encouragement." Still another shared this message: "Thank you for the thoughtful things you do. I don't have the same belief, but I appreciate yours."

Another person asked with a bit of a frustrated tone, "Why can't you just go to the store and buy cards?" In other words, "Why do you have to make the cards by hand?" I gently shook my head back and forth and said, "They wouldn't mean as much to them." Making the cards by hand speaks volumes. My neighbors see that I sacrifice my time, energy, and resources to show them kindness and love—God's love.

I can't believe I'm in my fourth year of the assignment! That is only possible with God's help, with His leading, direction, and provision. I am so blessed and humbled that He chose me for this assignment. What if I had not pursued an intimate relationship with Him? What if He hadn't invested time maturing me, making me a vessel He could use? What if I hadn't been willing to accept the assignment of making cards that show God's love to my neighbors? Only God knows what eternal impact my card ministry is having. If any of my neighbors want to know more about the God I love and serve, I am ready to talk to them. If they ask for help, I will be there.

A time for reflection

What I love about the neighboring movement is that it doesn't matter what age you are. Susan, a senior, is having an incredible impact with her neighbors. She points out something rather profound in her story—her mobile home park is her mission field. Generally, the perspective Christians have when they move into a new home is quite different from the perspective missionaries have when they move to their new country of ministry. When we look for a place to live, we generally look for a place that best suits us. Susan has a completely different perspective. Because most of us moved into our homes without a ministry mind-set, we need to re-inhabit them as missionaries do, as Susan did, by asking some of the following questions:

- Why does the Lord want me to live in this place?

- What is the Lord doing in this neighborhood?

- How does He want me to join Him?

- How can I best serve my neighbors?

- What are the needs of the people who live around me?

- What are my neighbors going through emotionally, and how can I help?

Respond

Make a list of simple things you can do for your neighbors to show them you care about them. Start praying through the list, asking God to lead you toward one of those simple things to show His love.

_____

_____

_____

_____

_____

_____

_____

_____

Susan Hanson lives in Southern California. She is the mother of one daughter and one son and a grandmother of a young adult grandson. Susan worked as a telephone operator receptionist, an elementary school librarian, and an ABA accredited paralegal administering trusts and estates. Now she is retired. She accepted the Lord at seven years old and was baptized at twelve. In midlife, when several life challenges hit, she cried out to the Lord wanting the abundant life He promised. She learned to listen to the Holy Spirit speak through His Word; to hear His still, small voice in prayer; and to be obedient to His leading.

17

Doing Good Gradually Opens Doors

> Let us not become weary in doing good, for at the proper time we will reap a harvest if we do not give up. Therefore, as we have opportunity, let us do good to all people, especially to those who belong to the family of believers. —Galatians 6:9–10

When our congregation started loving our neighbors, these verses were on a sign right outside the door where we would gather to pray before we would go out to care for our neighbors. We were going out weekly in groups to show the love of Jesus, and remarkable things were taking place. However, we were growing weary. But we didn't give up, and the Lord gradually opened the door for people to come into the kingdom. Carmen was one of those people. She experienced Jesus' love through a couple in our church, and her life was forever changed. Here is her story that she wrote soon after she gave her life to Jesus.

Carmen Jackson's Neighborhood

Deborah Santiago touched me and my mama deeply. We saw Deborah almost every day walking her rottweiler. Deborah was the neighborhood socialite. My mama, being a very sociable person herself and a rottweiler parent as well, ran out to talk to Deborah every time she saw her. My mama, Julia Castro, later introduced me to Deborah, and the three of us, and Deb's rotties, would stand outside and talk for fifteen to thirty minutes about our dogs or anything else that came to mind. Deborah often spoke about her church, the Valley Vineyard, and always invited us to the Sunday services and the women's tea. We always said that we would go to one of the Sunday services, but unfortunately we never did.

Mama and I were quite close, and we lived next door to each other. She died suddenly around the time I met Deborah. I was beside myself. I had lost my best friend and was grieving deeply. I reached out to Deborah asked her if she could recommend a pastor to speak at my mom's funeral, and she recommended Pastor Lynn Cory. I called him, we set up a meeting at the church, and Pastor Lynn asked me to bring some photos of my mama. I gathered up two bags' worth of photos, and I went through each one of them trying to give some history of each picture in between my tears of grief.

I talked for hours to Pastor Lynn about my beloved mama. He was so kind, compassionate, and understanding of the pain that I was going through that by the end of our meeting I felt as though I had known Lynn for over twenty years. He also mentioned he felt as though he had known my mom for many years. The three of us were no longer strangers, and I knew that Lynn was the perfect pastor to eulogize and give my mama her "Final Blessings."

"I'VE BECOME A CHRISTIAN, AND ALL OF THIS BECAUSE OF OUR WONDERFUL NEIGHBORS"

This was also the time that I met Neftali Santiago, Deborah's husband. He offered to create a video of music and pictures of my mama's life, and although he never met my mom, the way he put her Celebration of Life video together, you would swear that he had known her all his life. It was absolutely beautiful. I remember asking Neftali how much he thought the video was going to cost, and Neftali said, "Nothing, it's free." I remember thinking, *Who would do something this perfect and time consuming for free, especially since he did not know my mama or me?*

At this point I had only met three people who belonged to the Valley Vineyard, and they were like angels to me, but I didn't realize the power of God's love until I attended the women's tea in April of 2010. I finally went as Deborah Santiago's guest. I remember Sally O'Connor was the guest speaker. When she sang all I did was cry. I was so touched by her stories and how genuine she was. As a matter of fact, every woman I met that day was so sweet and caring that I thought there must be something special about this church. Since I was searching for God myself, I thought, *Why not?* I started going to church with Deborah, and although I was a little uncomfortable at first because I was used to a Catholic type of service, I found myself reading the Bible, loving God, and feeling great and as though I belonged.

About two months after my mama died, I was finally baptized, at age fifty-five, by Pastor Lynn and Pastor Bill. I remember going under the water as my old self and coming up out of the water as a completely different person, like the heavens opened up and the light of God surrounded me. I will never forget that feeling.

I'm a much better and happier person since I've become a Christian, and all of this because of our wonderful neighbors Neftali and Deborah Santiago, their love for God, and Deborah's love for her rotties and her neighbors.

A time for reflection

Carmen gave her life to the Lord and never looked back. She joined every class she could, got involved in a small group, helps with the teas, and shares her faith at work. One of my favorite things is to watch her worship wholeheartedly on Sunday mornings in our worship services. It all started with Deborah being herself and doing what she loved to do by walking and talking. In connecting with Carmen and her mom, one thing led to another, and God opened the door of her heart to Jesus. You can't make these things happen, but you can take the first step of doing good and seeing what God will do. Look at your neighborhood as a garden...start planting small seeds and see what grows. You will gradually reap a harvest if you don't give up.

Respond

Is there someone in your neighborhood that the Lord is prompting you to start a conversation with and to do some unexpected kind thing? Write down this person's name and what you would like to do for them.

_____

_____

_____

_____

Carmen Jackson was born in Balboa, Panama, where her father was stationed. She and her family moved to Southern California where she grew up. Carmen was not raised in a religious home. In 1977, Carmen joined the US Air Force/ Air National Guard and after 9/11 was deployed to Pakistan, where one of the chaplains invited her to go to one of the church services on base. She replied, "If I go to church, there will be an earthquake and the building will fall down." Carmen was baptized on Easter Sunday 2010. She still attends the Valley Vineyard and loves the Lord. The Valley Vineyard has not yet fallen down and is even stronger for Carmen being there.

18

God Showed Up

Ask the Lord of the harvest, therefore, to send out workers into his harvest field. —Matthew 9:38

Through the years, I have learned how important these words of Jesus' are. I have found that if I want to see God move in my neighborhood, I have had to be faithful in praying for my neighbors regularly. Through this regularity of prayer, God has made Himself evident through my neighbors' lives in surprising ways. I have found that prayer walking works best for me because it helps me focus when I pray. Prayer walking has also allowed me to connect with people in my own neighborhood more effectively than anything else has. While walking, I cross the path of neighbors who are walking with their children or taking their dogs for walks, and even with other adults on their own walks. It has opened the door to so many opportunities.

It took me years to learn the significance of prayer for my neighbors. This became obvious to me when I watched what God did in Domingo's neighborhood many years ago. It all started when Nadine Erickson and others began to pray for Domingo's neighborhood. Let's see what God did.

Domingo Cabral's Neighborhood

Neighborhood Initiative began in 2008 when we adopted eight square blocks around our church's facility. We called it Mission: Reseda back then. Today it has moved from the safety net of church ministry to our personally adopting neighborhoods where we live. Domingo Cabral lived on one of those eight blocks. A team of people was praying specifically for his neighborhood.

On the very evening we first started Mission: Reseda, a representative from the Los Angeles Neighborhood Housing Services walked into our church and asked our senior pastor Bill Dwyer and me if we would be interested in participating with others in the community to paint five homes. The timing was remarkable, but the location of the five homes was even more so. These homes were right in the neighborhoods that we were adopting. Approximately one hundred people from our church and two hundred from other service-oriented groups participated on that sunny day, and the Lord used that activity to open the hearts of neighbors in the community.

Domingo lived in one of those five homes. He came to the Lord while in prison and was looking for a church that did what Jesus did. He was taken aback by those from our church who showed him this kind of love, but he kept his distance to see if we were genuine. We told him we would help him trim his trees in the backyard, and when we followed through he began to realize that we were serious about being a presence in his community.

What also captured his attention was when he saw a young woman walking through his neighborhood with her children on several occasions. He wasn't sure what she was up to. Nadine Erickson, a woman from our church, had made a practice of praying through Domingo's neighborhood. She would take her four children on stroller rides throughout the neighborhood and pray for the neighbors. From those early days of prayer God has moved significantly in Domingo's neighborhood.

Within his neighborhood, we have hung Christmas lights, gone Christmas caroling, hosted major block parties, and held many free car washes. At one car wash, more than 100 people participated. Two Mormon missionaries from Utah, who lived in the neighborhood, were very excited about the whole experience. One of them said to me, "This is the most exciting thing I've seen since I've been in L.A.!"

"NOTHING HAPPENS WITHOUT PRAYER."

Domingo has since become very involved with our church and very committed to serving people in his neighborhood. He has painted the side of one of his neighbor's houses, helped build a driveway gate for another neighbor, helped put in a new sidewalk for another, and done many other things for his neighbors because of the love shown toward him. More importantly, he has developed meaningful relationships with many of his neighbors and has been there for them when they needed someone. Domingo and I have become best friends, and I was privileged to help him with a Bible study for his neighbors at his local Starbucks.

Ernesto, one of the neighbors in that small Bible study, now attends our Sunday gatherings because of his young daughter Valerie. She was probably only four years old at the time. There was something very special about Valerie and her unique love for the Lord. I am sure she was attracted by the love displayed by Domingo and this small group from our church that came into her neighborhood. Valerie was so touched by this love that she wanted to be a part of our church family. There was only one way for her to join us on Sunday mornings and that was for her dad to take her. He told me on different occasions, "I am here because of Valerie." Fast -forward nine years, Dad is still attending our services, and Valerie, now thirteen, has participated in Christmas plays, vacation Bible school, and is very active with our youth group. Whenever I see her, I receive a big hug…no words are needed. I am deeply touched by her humble spirit.

Valerie's story is one of many in Domingo's neighborhood. It all started with a group praying and a mother walking her four young children in a stroller and praying for people in Domingo's neighborhood, and then God showed up. Nadine knew that nothing happens without prayer…asking the Lord of the harvest to send out laborers into the harvest field.

A time for reflection

Do you think Nadine ever imagined all that would take place in Domingo's neighborhood by her simply taking her children on stroller rides and praying for those in his neighborhood? Her prayers, along with those of others, served to awaken believers to join together to participate in a remarkable work of God in Domingo's neighborhood. Domingo became the touchstone for change in his neighborhood. One life reached led to many other lives getting a taste of God's goodness. I will never forget when around one hundred people, young and old, were Christmas caroling in his neighborhood. I remember saying to my wife jo, "That was one of the highlights of my Christian experience." So many people were touched in his neighborhood that evening.

Have you considered walking through your neighborhood and praying for your neighbors as Nadine did and seeing what the Lord will do? I would encourage you to make it a part of the rhythm of your life, and watch and see how the Lord shows up in supernatural ways. This is the *kairos* adventure.

Respond

Often we think we have to do big things to make a difference in our neighborhood. How does this story encourage you to do something in your neighborhood no matter how small it may seem?

_____

_____

_____

_____

_____

Domingo Cabral grew up in Pasadena, California, and was highly influenced by the wrong element. His life was marked by dealing drugs, violence, and owning high-end cars. Domingo believed he was on the top of the world, but his life came crashing down when the police apprehended him and he landed in prison for four and a half years. During his incarceration, Domingo came to the Lord through reading the book of Job. When he got out, he lived humbly and was looking for a church that did what Jesus did. Today, he works as a parking attendant and shares his faith regularly.

19

God of the Impossible

Now to him who is able to do immeasurably more than
all we ask or imagine, according to his power that is at
work within us, to him be glory in the church and in
Christ Jesus throughout all generations, for ever and ever!
Amen. —Ephesians 3:20–21

Through the years, I have heard people in the Church say to me
something like this: "My neighbors are so difficult. Nothing could
ever happen in our neighborhood!" I listen quietly and try not to
offer trite solutions when people say how impossible it would be
to show this kind of love to their neighbors. I commit to pray for
them and those in their neighborhood. Why? Only God can shift
their perspective and the perspectives of their neighbors. Only
God can create opportunities that turn things around in a neighborhood. Yes, we can do unconditional acts of kindness that may
help with difficult neighbors, but it's God who changes hearts and
knows the hidden keys to unlock relationships.

David is a dear friend of mine. The first time I talked with him
about reaching out to his neighbors, he responded to me with,
"That will never happen in my neighborhood." I had a feeling this
"neighborhood thing" wasn't for him. However, I was quite surprised, to say the least, when one Thursday morning at one of our
weekly pastors' prayer gatherings, David shared this story.

David Cuff's Neighborhood

I met my neighbor Tom ten years ago right after I moved in next door to him. He told me he had been an alcoholic for more than forty years and had been sober for the previous two months.

A few weeks later while taking out my trash early in the morning, I noticed many undercover law enforcement vehicles in front of my house. The officers immediately exited their vehicles, and before I knew what was happening, Tom was handcuffed on his front lawn. As it turns out, they were serving a warrant for one of Tom's prior roommates. But when they asked me what I knew about Tom, I remember saying he was a nice neighbor and a sober alcoholic.

Over the years we had a friendly and casual relationship. During that time Alcoholics Anonymous became his life. Our church reached out to him by helping with his house projects, and I mowed and edged his lawns often. I shared the gospel with him many times, and he was always respectfully positive, but never had time to pray with me or come to church.

**"MY ONLY REGRET IS THAT I DID NOT
SPEND MORE TIME WITH HIM."**

Then Tom was diagnosed with liver cancer. I remember the first day he told me about it because he said it was his own fault for drinking for over forty years, and he didn't blame anyone. We prayed…and after his surgery it seemed evident that he was going to make it. He came over more often, and our relationship took a more personal and sensitive turn.

Then his liver cancer returned, and the doctor gave him two months to live. I remember making a point to spend more time with him when he told me. We invited Tom and his girlfriend of twenty years over for dinner and a swim. My family really made a special time for them. We went swimming and had dinner and dessert. Jim loved to go to the movies, so I took him to see *The Avengers*. Besides just wanting to show him a great time, I remember the feeling I had before taking him to the movies—one of urgency to share the gospel with him again. My wife said that he would probably bring it up, and before my car left the driveway he did. We had a great time, and Jim said he was ready to meet Jesus. Two weeks later, he died. My only regret is that I did not spend more time with him over the last ten years.

The video of David sharing this story is at http://neighborhoodinitiative.org. Click on the Resource tab and then on Videos.

A time for reflection

I like to believe that God can open doors into neighbors' lives in every neighborhood, even if it seems impossible. We tend to think nothing will change, but as we see in Tom's case, a dramatic change in life can change people's perspective. Of course, prayer is essential, and then hearts begin to open as we show our neighbors we care by investing some time with them and demonstrating God's love. David's closing statement, "My only regret is that I did not spend more time with him over the last ten years," is very captivating.

What is your response to that statement as it relates to your own neighbors? Do you view your neighborhood as David did? If yes, do you believe God can do the seemingly impossible in your neighbors' lives? If yes, how could He use you to bring that kind of change?

Respond

How would your attitude towards your neighbors change if you knew they only had six months to live? How can you maintain that type of attitude toward your neighbors at all times?

_____

_____

_____

_____

David Cuff grew up in the San Fernando Valley. After a successful career as a computer network engineer in Orange, California, he moved back to the neighborhood he grew up in and started a local church where he served faithfully for twenty years. He now serves as the president of Local View LLC, a digital marketing company assisting small and medium-sized businesses. David has been a significant help to me and Neighborhood Initiative since its inception. He has been married for thirty-five years and has three grown children and three grandchildren. David still loves his neighbors.

20

Mercy Triumphs over Judgment

> If you really keep the royal law found in Scripture, "Love your neighbor as yourself," you are doing right. But if you show favoritism, you sin and are convicted by the law as lawbreakers. For whoever keeps the whole law and yet stumbles at just one point is guilty of breaking all of it.... Speak and act as those who are going to be judged by the law that gives freedom, because judgment without mercy will be shown to anyone who has not been merciful. Mercy triumphs over judgment. —James 2:8–10, 12–13

One of the significant blemishes on the Church today is judgmentalism toward those outside the Church. James made a weighty point that should override the propensity of us Christians to make such judgments. Because we have been shown mercy, we of all people should in turn pass on that same mercy to everyone else. He pointed out that if we make distinctions by showing favoritism in loving our neighbors, then we sin and become a lawbreaker. Making these kinds of judgments and distinctions violates the royal law—loving your neighbor as yourself. In other words, if you close your heart to being merciful, then you close your heart to His mercy.

The same door through which the mercy of God will come into your heart and life, rescuing you, transforming you, and enabling you to live by the royal law, is the door through which that mercy must flow out to others. But if you slam that door shut because you don't like your neighbors because of the way they live their lives, or if you feel yourself to be morally superior to them, then you have slammed and locked the very door through which God's mercy was longing to come to you as well.[9] Now that may sound very severe, but it is true. Please know that I have made judgments of people more times than I would like to admit, but I am grateful that the Lord has rescued me many times from this foolishness because of His abounding mercy and grace.

One of my favorite stories was told to me by Andrew Burchett, pastor of Neighborhood Church in Chico, California. I don't know the couple's name—we'll call them the Parsons—but their story certainly needs to be heard by us who are in the Church today. They had to grapple with this very issue of making judgments about a couple in their neighborhood. Permit me to tell their story.

The Parson's Neighborhood

The Parsons were a part of Pastor Andrew's thriving church, and he was beginning to encourage those in the congregation to go out into their own neighborhoods and to love their neighbors. Andrew had made this a practice in his own neighborhood for many years, and he had grown up with parents who modeled this. He now wanted the whole congregation to do the same. So one Sunday this couple decided they too were going to set out to love their neighbors.

They expressed their love in a variety of ways. They began by giving gifts to different neighbors. They came across a couple in their neighborhood that was living together and not married. At first, it created a bit of tension for them, but after some consideration they decided to demonstrate love toward them by giving them a nice gift like they did to all the other neighbors.

"THE YOUNG COUPLE
WAS OVERJOYED WITH THE GIFT."

Sometime later the young couple became pregnant. When the mother delivered, the Parsons had real reservations about giving them a gift for their newborn child. After working through their uncertainties, they decided the right thing to do was to give the couple a nice gift. The young couple was overjoyed with the thoughtful gift.

Now here's the twist in the story. Sometime later, Mr. Parson had a stroke, and he was paralyzed on half of his body. He was no longer able to do his normal chores around the house and wondered how to manage this dilemma. Guess who began to mow the lawn each week and care for their needs? It was the young father. Can you imagine what would have happened if the Parsons had decided to exclude the young couple from their attempts at loving their neighbors?

I don't know the rest of the story. I would imagine that the couples struck up a wonderful relationship and one thing led to another because they chose mercy over judgment.

A time for reflection

Being judgmental is part of our human nature, but it is not how Jesus lived His life. If anyone had a right to be judgmental, it was Jesus, who lived a perfect life and is God. However, His words while He was on the cross—"Father, forgive them, for they do not know what they are doing" (Luke 23:23)—are a constant reminder to us in the Church that judgmentalism should not define us. We should be like Jesus, "full of grace and truth" (John 1:14). These were the qualities that attracted sinners to Him.

Respond

Do these qualities of Jesus characterize you when it comes to family, friends, and neighbors? If not, what would it take for the Holy Spirit to change this behavior? If yes, may your life continue to be an example to others of Jesus' gracious life.

21

Compassion Knows No Bounds

Jesus went through all the towns and villages, teaching in their synagogues, proclaiming the good news of the kingdom and healing every disease and sickness. When he saw the crowds, he had compassion on them, because they were harassed and helpless, like sheep without a shepherd. —Matthew 9:35–36

Jesus made it abundantly clear to His disciples why He had such compassion for the crowds. He viewed the multitudes like harassed and helpless sheep without a shepherd. He gave this comparison because the disciples knew full well what it meant for sheep to be without a shepherd. Those of us who don't spend time with sheep are unaware of how grave it is for sheep to be left alone. Without a shepherd, domestic sheep will die. If a sheep falls over on its back, it can't right itself. Sheep are defenseless animals and are so fearful that a stray jackrabbit will cause a flock of sheep to stampede. Without a shepherd, there is extreme tension among sheep...like we see among people in our cities today.

However, when the shepherd walks up to the sheep all of this tension stops, and they focus on the shepherd. Jesus intended to help His disciples, and us, to understand the human condition without the Good Shepherd. When I picture a sheep, I imagine an innocent, maybe even cute, animal. People in our neighborhoods, without Jesus, may not seem to be innocent or nearly as endearing. Matt's story invites us to see that even if we lack compassion, God is fully able to transform our perspective.

Matt and Jourdan Svajda's Neighborhood

Have you ever been frustrated by a neighbor? I was getting so frustrated by the appearance of my neighbor's house as it sat just a short walk down my sidewalk; it was clear that he didn't take care of his home whatsoever. This guy frustrated me, and I hadn't even met him yet! Trash lay everywhere in the overgrown, weedy yard. The fence that separated the front and backyards was thrashed, and the neighbors next door were even complaining. The beat-up car in the driveway had a few flat tires and clearly had been sitting there for a long time. Needless to say, it was a mess, and every time I walked past the house, frustration grew in me as I noticed new problems compounding. His house was the only one disrupting the perfectly put-together little community we lived in. I wanted to write this person off as a "lost cause" and send the city after him for making our neighborhood look bad and causing our street's real estate values to tumble.

But then one day as I was walking by his house, glancing in contempt, it was as if God asked me the question, *Do you think I have love for this neighbor of yours?* The question immediately paused my walk. As I processed, it was obvious I knew that God did in fact care for my neighbor and didn't judge him because of his housing situation; obviously, I couldn't say the same. In fact, I judged and drew conclusions about his entire life, and we hadn't even met. That day I walked past his house feeling convicted as my perspective was beginning to change. I now had a small seed of compassion toward him and wanted to get to know him. Then shortly thereafter, these four simple words changed my entire perspective about my neighbor Omid: tell me your story.

"TELL ME YOUR STORY."

I invited Omid over for lunch, another day for dinner, and then another day for a potluck. Before I knew it, Omid was becoming a regular as his life started overlapping with ours. I learned that he was a single, fifty-five-year-old Iranian man with a Muslim background. He shared how economic times had hit him hard and how the city had even been contacting him with phone calls and letters about his home. His feeling of losing hope in himself compounded daily, and the more I learned his story, the more I felt for him and his situation. So, I decided to do something about it.

One day as I sat on his couch, I asked Omid, "Would you allow me to give you a hand around your house? I'd love to serve you, and I have some friends who would as well." His immediate response was no, but he also asked, "Why?" I pointed out that I was a Christian and that my role in this world is to love my God with everything I have and then to love my neighbor as much as myself. I then said, "You're my neighbor." It took him a bit, but I got a call from Omid the next week as he accepted my offer. I shared his story with my life group, and we raised close to a thousand dollars in a couple days.

So, one Sunday morning from about 7:00 a.m. to 1:00 p.m., our life group "skipped church" to serve my neighbor. We landscaped his yard, built him a fence, and hauled away a ton of stuff to a rented garbage bin. Around 10:00 a.m. Omid came up to me and said, "Matt! Why are you here?" A bit confused, I looked at him and said, "What do you mean?" "Why aren't you at church? It's Sunday!" he said. I paused a second, pointed to my friends, and declared, "Omid, this is the Church."

It took him a moment to process before replying to me in a soft, humbled voice, "I'm ready to hear about Jesus now." So, I told him my story and the gospel story. I told him how much God loved him. Over the coming months we met weekly in our neighborhood park to read God's Word together.

The children's show host Mister Rogers once said, "You'll never meet a person you can't learn to love once you've heard their story." These words are so true. Hearing and understanding Omid's story helped me to begin to see Omid as a person instead of a problem. Omid even gave his life to Christ shortly thereafter. I'm so humbled that God would still use me in my selfishness and brokenness. Little did I recognize how God was already at work and drawing Omid to Himself. He allowed me to participate in His redemption story, and I'm grateful for that.

A time for reflection

Like Matt, I have made superficial judgments of neighbors based on the way they have taken care of their home or property. But when I have gotten to know them and heard their story, often my view of them has changed. How about you? Have you made premature judgments about neighbors without getting to know them? Are you open to the possibility of God changing the way you see someone whose behavior is bothering you? Is the Lord asking you a similar question, like He did Matt: Do you think *I have love for this neighbor of yours?* Maybe it's time to get to know this neighbor or even put a team together to help this neighbor with their home or property.

Respond

Is there someone in your neighborhood whom you have judged based on outward appearance? What steps could you take to get to know this neighbor better, and if that neighbor has a need, how could you help him or her?

_____

_____

_____

_____

Matt Svajda and his wife, Jourdan, and three kids live on the Space Coast of Florida where God moved them to live as salt and light in their community. They run a ministry called Fiducia (fiduciacommunity.com) that helps activate the everyday Christian to live out their faith where they live, work, and play. They also lead a neighborhood-focused home church where neighbors like Omid can experience being part of the family of God.

22

The Power of Transparency

Take my yoke upon you and learn from me, for I am gentle and humble in heart, and you will find rest for your souls. For my yoke is easy and my burden is light.
—Matthew 11:29–30

Humility is one of the finer qualities that we can exhibit to our neighbors. We see it so clearly demonstrated in the life of our Savior. We Christians at times can come off to those in our neighborhoods like we have it all together. However, one day we might find ourselves in a place where it becomes clear to us that we in fact fall quite short of having it all together. Nothing is more humbling than to realize that we said or did something that requires open and honest confession with one of our neighbors. There is power in this kind of open confession, and you will see it displayed in Annette's story.

Annette Grable's Neighborhood

There is nothing like the power of transparency to redeem.

Many years ago, I began babysitting my neighbors' children. They were preschoolers when I started, and I have forever loved these girls I call "my Monday-through-Friday, 9-to-5 daughters." I took them everywhere with my kids, and they were family.

Except for one thing. I was living with a years-old spirit of poverty. Even though I was no longer poor, the life of lack I'd previously experienced still had a significant grip on me. This mentality manifested itself like this: my neighbor very generously brought food over each day, enough for her kids and mine, while I made food for my kids only. I greedily thought of my neighbor's contribution to meals as part of my pay. With a bitter heart, I didn't share our food. Fortunately, my mentality had little impact when the girls were young and unaware of what my experience brought to our relationship. The girls really had no clue and my kids didn't see the issue. I didn't discuss it with them or anyone because I thought I was simply being rational.

Fast-forward to when the girls started noticing that there was the food they brought and shared, and the food I never shared. I can't remember my responses when they'd asked why. Probably, it was the way I covered myself with the cloud that poverty from my past left over me.

"FOR ME THERE WAS THAT NAGGING CONVICTION"

Around the same time, we had made new family friends from our then new church. I can still hear the wife, a best friend to me still, saying, "Have anything you want," about food in her house. I asked myself why I couldn't be like that too.

These feelings brewed and stewed in me a long time—so long, my neighbors' girls grew into young adults. Maybe that's just how long God needed to let it bother me to the point of conviction.

It never strained our relationship as neighbors, and I often felt such warmth toward them that the girls' mom was like a sister to me. We'd been through a lot together. We supported each other, attended the same get-togethers, did Girl Scout events together, shared patio furniture for parties, had yard sales together, and had regular girls' nights out with our daughters.

But still, for me there was a nagging conviction, and I knew God wanted me to make it right. Being a good neighbor wasn't enough. It also wasn't enough to just share food to make up for the past. So, as it weighed on me, I prayed about what would be a redeeming blessing.

These neighbors are wonderful friends. The mom started a Girl Scout troop when the girls and my daughter were little, and it led to a circle of friends that included us and continues to this day. These neighbors are a galvanizing force. I don't think this circle of friends would exist if it weren't for them and their hospitality.

Hospitality. That was the answer. I knew they could use a new BBQ with all the entertaining they did. I waited for a really good sale that my wallet could handle and bought them a grill. It wasn't the fanciest or the best money could buy, but it was what I could do. I hoped it would last a while and provide many good meals.

After I bought the grill, I went to their door, and my friend answered. I said I had something heavy I needed help with in the back of my car, a gift for them, and that they couldn't say no. She looked puzzled as she listened to my story.

I really had to work hard to hold back the waterworks and explain in terms that made sense. *Spirit of poverty* and *greed* are not words of everyday conversation. I explained that God had been working on my spirit for years, to change my heart to one of generosity and to redeem my behavior from so many years ago. I asked that they would forgive me and accept this small token of redemption. My friend was very surprised, and by the end of my explanation, we were both teary-eyed as I thanked her for listening.

Now years later, the grill sits in a prominent corner of their yard surrounded by plants. It's no longer useful as a grill because the bottom burned out. But still, it's there and hasn't been replaced. I don't know why.

But what I do know is that every time I see it, it's my marker for an overdue moment of transparency, my reminder of redemption, the testimony of a broken spirit of poverty that was replaced by a spirit of generosity.

A time for reflection

Whatever perception people may have of Christians trying to look good on the outside, when someone like Annette allows Jesus to permeate her own life, it speaks volumes about what Christianity really is: the power of God to redeem every broken thing in us. Her beautiful story portrays something that none of us likes to do. Who wants to go to a neighbor (or whoever) and expose something that has been hidden in our hearts that needs to be made right? However, confession is good for the soul and has the power to transform a life as it did Annette's. Is the Lord speaking to you through Annette's story?

Respond

Is there someone who you need to make things right with? Humbling yourself is not an easy thing to do, and in some cases, it takes time. Is now the time to make things right? Write down some tangible steps you can take to surrender to God and move in the direction He is leading you.

_____

_____

_____

_____

Reared by family and friends in Los Angeles; the San Fernando Valley; Modesto, California; and Mexico—and having attended six elementary and two middle schools—Annette Grable begged for stability. She and her husband, Kevin, provided that anchor for their own family, living in the same Studio City neighborhood more than thirty years in the home Kevin grew up in. They considered moving to Seattle or Denver when their kids were little, but that wasn't God's plan. They love their neighborhood and put on a Halloween event each year, passing out over two hundred free hot dogs and providing coffee, hot chocolate, and candy.

23

Things Aren't Always What They Seem

Don't you have a saying, "It's still four months until harvest"? I tell you, open your eyes and look at the fields! They are ripe for harvest. —John 4:35

Jesus, in this verse, was trying to convey to His disciples that they didn't see what He was seeing, something that was right before them. They were looking in one dimension, and He was seeing things in a completely different dimension. Their eyes were trained on natural things—the fields that were four months until the time of harvest—but Jesus saw the spiritual dimension—people who were approaching Him and were ripe for spiritual harvesting. We may be humored at times by the disciples' inability to see what Jesus saw, but more than we would like to admit, we see things incorrectly as well. We judge neighbors or people we see in the market when we don't have the full picture. We just don't have a clue. It is humbling to find that what we thought about someone is not true at all. I am sure we all can identify with Chris's story.

Chris Anthony Lansdowne's Neighborhood

I was standing in a long line at a children's toy store to buy a gift for my neighbor's son's birthday party. I couldn't help but feel annoyed with how long the line was, and how slow it was moving. The longer the wait took, the more frustrated I became. I'm not proud of my attitude, but I wasn't in a real happy mood, waiting in a long line at a toy store.

Finally, I got close to the front of the line, and just happened to notice the guy working at the cash register. He was keeping his head down, not acknowledging the customers as they laid their purchases in front of him. Head down, he scanned the toys, put them in bags, and never said a word.

No eye contact. No "How are you?" No "Have a nice day." No, "Sorry for the long line." He was pretty much just going through the motions.

I thought, *Wow, this is terrible customer service; someone should really say something to him. That's not how you treat your customers.* I'm a very complimentary person when it comes to someone doing a good job. In fact, I'll even call over the manager to sing their praises, but this was less than praiseworthy.

I thought I might even be helping him, by mentioning to him how he should make more of an effort to be pleasant and make eye contact with his customers.

So, when my turn came at the cash register, I leaned in a little close, so as not to embarrass him, and whispered, "Having a bad day?" hoping that would somehow jolt him into being aware of his noticeable mood.

"I NEED TO SEE PAST WHAT MY EYES SEE."

As if in slow motion, he picked up his head and said, "Yes, I am. My mom is very sick and is in the hospital, and she might die."

It was as if a huge foot came crashing into my stomach. I felt weak in the knees, and a horrible guilt immediately set in. "I am soooo sorry to hear that," I said. His words so affected my heart, I just froze. Shame on me, for not once thinking that perhaps this poor kid might be suffering in some way. He was hurting and just trying to cope.

I walked around to him at the cash register, and with open arms, I hugged him, and he hugged me back with a brokenness and a surrender I've never felt before. I said, "I'm so sorry. I will pray for you and your mama."

How could I so easily forget that there is a hurting world out there? I need to see past what my eyes see and look with my heart. So many people need to be asked, "How are you?" No, I don't mean the "How are you?" that is just being polite, but the kind of question that wants to really hear how they are. How many need us to connect with them, care, and say, "Your life matters"?

A time for reflection

Loving one's neighbor is not just for the neighbor next door, but for those who cross our path throughout the day. Like Chris, we all have experienced what she experienced while waiting in line at a market or store. Can you remember going through a situation like what Chris experienced? How did you handle it? How does Chris's story help you to reconsider making personal judgments about neighbors or those at the market?

Respond

What is one thing that jumped out at you from this story? How can you be more attentive to the needs of others in your community?

_____

_____

_____

_____

_____

Chris Anthony Lansdowne is an American voice actress best known as host of Focus on the Family's Adventures in Odyssey. *As host of the program for more than three decades, she is heard weekly on more than two thousand radio stations worldwide. She was the longest-running voice of Barbie and is a friend to millions upon millions of little kids everywhere.*

24

Listening Is Counterintuitive

My dear brothers and sisters, take note of this: Everyone should be quick to listen, slow to speak and slow to become angry, because human anger does not produce the righteousness that God desires. —James 1:19–20

Genuine listening is a virtue. Very few people are good at it today, but when you come across someone who is, it's hard not to value the rare treasure you've found. My good friend David Sanford asked me to read the manuscript of his book *Loving Your Neighbor: Surprise! It's Not What You Think.* I was captivated by the idea he conveyed that much of how we can be relating to neighbors is counterintuitive, that is, contrary to our intuition or common sense. Listening to neighbors, without interrupting them during the flow of their story, certainly differs from what we normally do in conversation. We tend to want to interject something. For instance, when someone is sharing something about herself we like to say something like, "That reminds me of _____," or, "I had that same experience." We think we are relating to what she is saying, but actually we are hijacking the story to talk about ourselves or something that we think is more significant than what she is saying. When we allow someone to tell her whole story without interrupting, we speak volumes. We are communicating that what she is saying is important. In fact, we are communicating that she has worth.

Listening is a door into a person's heart. David Sanford answered the following significant question in his chapter on listening: "How do we get today's generation interested in God's stories? By genuinely being interested in hearing their stories. Loving by listening. And listening some more. Without saying anything. Not a word."[10] His chapter on listening spoke to me, and here's what happened the following day.

Lynn and jo Cory's Neighborhood

The morning after I read that chapter, I walked out my front door just as my neighbor, Michael, walked out his front door. So, I strolled across the street. We stood on his sidewalk chatting for a few minutes. Then, Michael started to tell me at length about his wife's upbringing, her family, and much more. I thought about what I had read from David's book the day before. Instead of doing what I might normally have done, I did what was counterintuitive. I just listened, without interruption.

"I JUST LISTENED, WITHOUT INTERUPTION."

I didn't interject my own comments or try to identify with the story. So, Michael completely opened up and shared his wife's experiences in detail. It took nearly an hour. When he was done,

Michael said, "Lynn, thanks for listening to my story." I could tell it really meant a lot to him. Then Michael corrected himself: "Actually, that wasn't my story. That was Melody's story." I replied, "Michael, the next time we get a chance to talk, I'd like to hear your story."

Much of this chapter on listening and my story is taken from David Sanford's book Loving Your Neighbor: Surprise! It's Not What You Think.

A time for reflection

That experience undeniably confirmed that when we listen, people open up like a flower and really express what's on their hearts. If we interrupt, however, it stops the flow of what they're saying. Listening is a discipline. It isn't easy to do. We think we have something equal or better to say, or we want to ask a question. But often our neighbor isn't ready to be questioned. He or she is in the flow of thought. So, we need to let that neighbor keep talking until it's all out.

David is right. This is very counterintuitive. Granted, there's a place to ask questions. Then when answers start to come, we need to quiet down and let people talk until they've said everything they want to say. I walked away from the conversation with Michael confident that he felt heard and that he would be willing to talk again. Why? Because I was willing to listen and not interrupt him.

In our day, we pay big bucks to hire a counselor to listen to us without interrupting. Other people aren't willing to listen like that. They really aren't. That's the secret. I think when we listen, people become more vulnerable and willing to open up and talk, if they know they have someone who genuinely cares enough to listen to them. Let's do just that! Do you find yourself hijacking other people's stories, or have you experienced others interrupting you when you share yours? The next time someone begins to share his or her story, practice the discipline of listening. Like a muscle, the more you exercise it the better and stronger it gets.

Respond

Listening starts with asking good questions. Throughout the Gospels you will find that Jesus was always asking timely questions that opened doors for Him to listen and so much more. This week begin to ask thoughtful questions and then listen and observe how doors open in your relationship with a neighbor, family member, or friend.

David Sanford coaches leaders passionate about demonstrating the relevance of Jesus Christ in every major sphere of life. His books and Bible projects have been published by Zondervan, Tyndale, Thomas Nelson, Doubleday, and Amazon. His speaking engagements have ranged everywhere from the University of California, Berkeley, to the Billy Graham Center at The Cove, North Carolina.

25

Being Wise with Difficult Neighbors

Be wise in the way you act toward outsiders; make the most of every opportunity. Let your conversation be always full of grace, seasoned with salt, so that you may know how to answer everyone. —Colossians 4:5–6

Now and then we will be faced with neighbors who are intentionally difficult. They may not like the fact that we are Christians or that we appear to them to be "do-gooders." The most problematic situations may arise when we try to kindly ask if they can do something about, let's say, their annoying barking dog or loud music. Things like this can test us to the limits. Our first inclination may be to call the police. But the apostle Paul said, "If it is possible, as far as it depends on you, live at peace with everyone...Do not be overcome by evil, but overcome evil with good" (Romans 12:18, 21). It is so common for us Christians to turn to our own tactics with a maddening neighbor rather than to turn the other cheek (Matthew 5:38–39). Dave and Carrie were challenged greatly by just such a neighbor, and had many opportunities to abandon the above scriptures. Let's see how they handled the situation.

Dave and Carrie Irving's Neighborhood

Ironically, we moved to Reseda, a multi-ethnic, low-income neighborhood, because we wanted to "love our neighbors." In the '90s, most people were moving out of Reseda to the suburbs as soon as they could afford it. But we had just returned from Mexico (where we served as missionaries), and we felt God wanted us to continue to be missionaries, living just two blocks from our church in the heart of this particular neighborhood.

We did all the "right" things—had a block party, introduced ourselves, invited our neighbors to a Bible study (in Spanish) at our home, had yearly neighborhood teas, gave out Christmas goodies, knew the names of every neighbor, and tried to stay connected. And for the first few years, everything seemed to go well. We endured the nightly police helicopters flying overhead, the constant flow of cars stopping at the drug dealer's house across the street, the ranchero music playing until all hours of the night, the graffiti scratched into our fence, the stones that the neighborhood kids threw into our pool…It was all worth it. It was all part of "loving" our neighbors, we thought.

But one night, our next-door neighbor (we'll call him Bob) was playing his party music until two in the morning to the point where our windows were literally shaking. So, the next day when it all started again at two in the afternoon, my wife went over and asked him (kindly) to turn it down as she'd reached her limit. He chased her off the property, and from then on all hell broke loose. Anytime we had people over, he played music from giant speakers over our fence and played it so loud we couldn't have a conversation in our own backyard. That went on for over a year. Graduation parties, family get-togethers, and pool times were all ruined by his on-going amped-up music. He called animal control to come get our "vicious" dog (a playful boxer) when the dog ran up and down the fence line as he teased it. He claimed to smell car-paint fumes and had our property inspected by the city for illegal auto body work. He called the police to have us move our car which was "blocking" his driveway. He basically found whatever he could to harass and intimidate us. What once had been a friendly, neighborly relationship had turned into an all-out one-sided war against us.

After each incident, we tried to forgive and forget. We knew God was calling us to love our enemy. But how do you love someone who seems to hate you so much? We feel bad that things didn't turn out all rosy. Not a guilty, shaming kind of feeling bad. But a "Rats! We missed a great opportunity!" kind of feeling bad. I think loving our neighbors is a big part of who God is making us to be. It's a big part of becoming fully us! That's why Jesus told us it's the second most important commandment (Matthew 22:39). And it's why it's totally worth it to do the hard work of actively loving our neighbors. It's a lot more than being "nice" neighbors. It's all those hard things in 1 Corinthians 13: love never stops being patient, never stops believing, never stops hoping, and never gives up.

"RATS! WE MISSED A GREAT OPPORTUNITY!"

Two days before we loaded the U-Haul and left Reseda, we had a garage sale. We also put up a big sign that said, "Come say good-bye to the Irvings!" We had doughnuts and coffee, and throughout the morning we said our good-byes to all our neighbors and gave each other hugs. Just as we were taking things down, Bob came over. He made an attempt at small talk and kind of kicked at the dirt. And then he looked at me and said, "Four months ago I was diagnosed with brain cancer. I've been going through chemotherapy, but the doctors say I only have a few months to live." I was shocked! I put my arm around him and asked if I could pray for him. I genuinely cared about Bob. We prayed. We cried.

Three months later, we got the news that Bob had died.

Paul wrote, "Be wise in the way you act toward outsiders; make the most of every opportunity" (Colossians 4:5). As we get to know our new neighbors, Bob's memory serves as a constant reminder to truly love (initiate real relationship with) them.

A time for reflection

Who would have imagined that Dave and Carrie's story would have turned out the way it did with their neighbor? Dave's last conversation with Bob was extremely moving with Dave praying for him and tears flowing. The Lord has a way of softening even the hardest heart. I am grateful that Dave and Carrie continued to forgive Bob and to forget the torturous things he did to them through the years. I am sure Bob would never have approached Dave the way he did without having experienced the unconditional love of the Lord through them consistently throughout their years as neighbors.

Dave's sentiment—"Rats! We missed a great opportunity!"—may be a thought we also have had when a neighbor moved from our neighborhood or passed away. It's not too late to touch the lives of your neighbors who are still living next door to you. Paul said, "Make the most of every opportunity." The action He invites you into may look just like what the Irvings modeled for

Bob: patience and restraint. Be encouraged that it will not be in vain. Join the Father as He works in your neighbors' hearts and you show them the grace of God.

Respond

What opportunity is the Lord giving you with a neighbor, even if it is a difficult one?

_____

_____

_____

_____

_____

Dave and Carrie Irving live in Coeur d'Alene, Idaho. They have three grown children. They have ministered together for twenty-five years at the Valley Vineyard in Reseda, California, and as missionaries in Mexico.

26

Watch What You Say

Let your conversation be always full of grace, seasoned
with salt, so that you may know how to answer everyone.
—Colossians 4:6

In the above short verse, the apostle Paul pointed out two important virtues that should accompany our communication with those
outside the faith, especially with those who are belligerent. First,
he signified that we should let our words be gracious. Simply, we
are to let our words be kind and without judgment so we bring
out the best in others. And second, our words should be "seasoned
with salt, so that [we] may know how to answer everyone." Along
with showing grace, we need to be willing to take advantage of
opportunities to speak the truth wisely with neighbors who believe differently than us. These two virtues characterized Jesus; He
was "full of grace and truth" (John 1:14). We need to exhibit these
qualities in both word and deed with our neighbors. Mike demonstrated this beautifully with one of his neighbors who had had it
with God and church.

Mike and Mary Day's Neighborhood

In 2008 my fiancée and I started a neighborhood group in North Hills, California, for open Bible study. We also hosted neighborhood events we called Agape dinners, which featured local musicians. We typically drew five to ten people for the Bible studies, but the dinners proved very popular, bringing up to two dozen neighbors over to the house for fellowship, conversation, and good music.

Our neighbors were a decidedly mixed group socio-economically, some with a Christian background and many with little or no religious association. There were no other churchgoers in this group, the common bond being we were all neighbors. The group grew as we completed service projects in the neighborhood like washing neighbors' cars on the weekend and planning block parties.

"I WAS DETERMINED TO LOVE THIS MAN."

One young, married, professional couple that lived a couple of doors down from us were active and eager participants in this group even though they were emphatically non-Christian. I believe they were drawn into the group for two reasons: we were doing good things for neighbors without asking anything in return, and we did not push our faith on anyone. This couple had degrees in science, and the husband was a lapsed and somewhat angry Lutheran. His speech was often marked by critical and contemptuous remarks toward Christians, the Bible, the Church, and church leaders. And he was always spoiling for an argument concerning religion. I was determined to love this man, to model biblical Christianity to the best of my ability, to not blow my chance to witness my faith to them, and above all to stay out of pointless and unproductive arguments.

Our group planned a Thanksgiving food drive in the neighborhood, and we all participated. By all standards it was wildly successful and provided one of our local food pantries with cash and hundreds of dollars' worth of food for distribution. The shock and amazement the group experienced at the abundant response was incredible, and my fiancée and I saw God moving in our neighborhood.

My church held a Thanksgiving Eve service, and I was asked to teach. Part of my message included sharing the progress of our neighborhood group, so I went out on a limb and asked this couple to attend. I did this not so much for them to hear my teaching, but so that they would get up and share their experience at the food drive. They agreed to attend, and much to my surprise, the husband did the sharing, which he did skillfully. What also stands out in my mind was his obvious and visible discomfort during my teaching. I fully expected him to stand up and start arguing with me at any moment. It seemed to me the height of irony that my chosen text was the Parable of the Prodigal Son.

The group continued meeting and serving, and about a year later this young neighbor couple sold their house in the San Fernando Valley and moved to L.A. proper to be closer to work. Like most folks who relocate, they held a garage sale the week before they moved, and there was quite an array of books, clothes, tools, and tchotchkes on display. I walked down to their house to hang out and see if there was anything on offer I couldn't live without, and to help them out a bit financially.

I took a seat in the garage, and we started to chat. The husband kept making pointed, critical remarks about a vindictive, vengeful, angry, impetuous God and an error-ridden Bible. Clearly, he wanted to argue. For some reason, the book *The Bait of Satan* by John Bevere came to mind. I felt I was being "baited" into an argument in which I chose not to participate. How awkward.

My apparent indifference to his remarks eventually had an effect and he relaxed. After a bit, he fished a couple of familiar-looking books out of one stack and handed them to me. He said, "I figure you might have some use for these, and I'd like to give them to you, no charge!" The books were a Lutheran *Book of Worship* (hymnal) and his Bible from confirmation class all those years ago. I asked him if he was sure, and he said yes, he would no longer be needing them. I told him I would love to have them and they would stay in my possession until he wanted them back.

The stunned look on his face was genuine, and he said that would never happen. I gave him an equally genuine smile and told him I was pretty sure he would want them back one day and that I would keep them safe until he did. It was pretty much the first time I saw this intelligent, belligerent man with nothing to say. He hasn't contacted me yet, but I will never give up hope.

A time for reflection

After Mike sent me his story, he texted me and said, "Well, it's not a barn-burner success story, but it's all about planting seeds and watering, eh? It will be a heckuva story when he eventually wants [the books] back." I texted back, saying, "If all were barn-burner success stories the book wouldn't be authentic. The Bible is filled with stories like yours—the Rich Young Ruler is a perfect example." He responded, "So true."

Don't let someone in your neighborhood discourage you, but have the kind of hope that Mike has, that God is responsible for the outcome. Mike understood that his part was just to plant and water. But in addition to that, he offered words seasoned with salt. Just as salt has the ability to enhance taste and preserve, our speech can offer a taste of the truth of the gospel and keep it preserved until the time God has prepared. Do you have a neighbor like this who is resistant? If yes, how can you demonstrate the kind of grace the apostle Paul encouraged?

Respond

How do you measure success when it comes to neighboring?

_____

_____

_____

_____

Mike Day is a retired cinetechnician and pastor currently residing in Lompoc, California. A native of Oshkosh, Wisconsin, Mike earned a bachelor of science degree at Portland State University and a masters of arts in theology from Fuller Theological Seminary. Employed for thirty-three years in Los Angeles film studios, Mike now owns and operates KTNK, a radio station broadcasting out of Lompoc. Mike lives with his wife, Mary, and has three children—Mike, Lindsay, and Demarie. Besides doing part-time pastoral work, Mike plays dobro in a bluegrass band called Too Little Too Late.

27

Timing Is Everything

Devote yourselves to prayer, being watchful and thankful. And pray for us, too, that God may open a door for our message, so that we may proclaim the mystery of Christ, for which I am in chains. Pray that I may proclaim it clearly, as I should. Be wise in the way you act toward outsiders; make the most of every opportunity. Let your conversation be always full of grace, seasoned with salt, so that you may know how to answer everyone.
—Colossians 4:2–6

I am sure you have heard the old expression, "Timing is everything." Solomon offered further advice about timing: "Like apples of gold in settings of silver is a word spoken in right circumstances" (Proverbs 25:11, NASB). Timing and right circumstances are essential to sharing the gospel with a neighbor. The apostle Paul gave additional clarity as to when the Lord wants us to speak to someone about Him: "And pray for us, too, that God may open a door for our message." There needs to be a heart that is open to the gospel message.

We have either experienced firsthand or observed someone else sharing the gospel with an individual who is not ready for it. It is like force-feeding a child; it doesn't work. Actually, it does more harm than good. On the other hand, we may have found ourselves walking away from a conversation and realizing that we missed a significant opportunity. That's why Paul said, "Pray that I may proclaim it clearly, *as I should.*" Paul was human like the rest of us, and, believe it or not, could have missed out on an opportunity that the Lord may have given him. Let's observe how Alan waited for a God-given opportunity (*kairos*).

Alan Doswald's Neighborhood

A few years ago, a seventy year-old man (let's call him Joe) moved in across the street from us, and we became friends. As we began building a relationship with him, we realized he had no interest in hearing about the Lord. However, we continued to share about our own lives and our relationship with Jesus as the Lord led us to.

Then the Lord opened a door. During one of our conversations, I mentioned to Joe that my wife had written a book. He said he would to like to read it. It just so happens that the purpose of her book is to clearly lay out the gospel message in an easy-to-understand way.

"THIS IS THE MOMENT I'VE BEEN WAITING FOR MY ENTIRE LIFE."

It is designed for those who know little about Jesus, and it brings them to a point where they can make an intelligent decision about accepting Christ as their Savior. So one day, after reading my wife's book, Joe told me he wanted to be "reborn again," baptized, and go to a Protestant church. I asked him, "When?" and he replied, "Right now." So we walked across the street to our house where my wife and I led him to Christ. After he prayed to receive Christ, he leaned back in his chair and said, "This is the moment I've been waiting for my entire life." He was then baptized and began attending church with us when he was able to physically.

Then his health began to decline so he was unable to attend church, and he moved across town. So we visited him regularly at his new house and continued to disciple him there. He calls us his "pastors," and we've had the privilege of watching Joe grow in the Lord over the years. God has turned his life around, and his relatives see the difference. Over the years we have attended several of his family gatherings, and they have welcomed us almost as though we were part of their family. We have discovered that our neighbors are connected to others who we can also love.[11]

Alan's story is from his book *Pray and Do the Next Thing*.

A time for reflection

If Alan would have imposed the gospel on Joe, Joe more than likely would have been turned off, and his network of relationships that were touched later never would have been reached. Joe's statement, "This is the moment I've been waiting for my entire life," says it all. Timing (*kairos*) is everything if we are to share the gospel with a receptive heart. Early on, Joe was in no way ready, but God prepared his heart in time through conversation and relationship with Alan and his wife.

Kairos can be both the opportunity that presents itself, where all the lesser things fade away into the one thing in front of you, and a longer appointed time set by God where you sow and He opens hearts to Him. Jesus told His disciples to follow Him and He would make them fishers of men. I am sure one of the things that He emphasized was patience. If you have done any fishing, you know that you must patiently wait for fish to bite. I like that Alan didn't give up on Joe when he implied he was uninterested in hearing about the Lord. Alan waited until the timing was right.

Respond

Is there a family member, friend, or a neighbor who has expressed to you they have no interest in the Lord, but they like you? Do you need to revisit this relationship and wait on the Lord to open that person's heart? Who might that be, and what direction would the Lord like you to take with that person?

_____

_____

_____

_____

_____

Alan Doswald is the author of Pray and Do the Next Thing *and has served in full-time Christian ministry in Fresno, California, since 1972. He served in Youth for Christ for ten years. Then in 1982, the Lord led him to found and direct Evangelicals for Social Action (ESA) in Fresno, where he currently serves to mobilize churches to help people in need. During that time he also served as a consultant for World Vision for fifteen years and helped many cities across the United States. In addition, he developed Love INC, which organizes churches to work together to serve their communities.*

28

Six Couples
Meeting House to House

They devoted themselves to the apostles' teaching and to
fellowship, to the breaking of bread and to prayer....They
broke bread in their homes and ate together with glad
and sincere hearts, praising God and enjoying the favor
of all the people. And the Lord added to their number
daily those who were being saved. —Acts 2:42, 46–47

Six neighborhood couples meet monthly from house to house for
Sunday dinner and to pray for their neighbors. Around thirty-four
neighbors live in their immediate community. Wouldn't it be great
if a dinner and prayer time like this were going on in every neighborhood around our country? Shawn and Carla's story is reminis-
cent of the first-century Church—brothers and sisters of different
backgrounds, gathering together in love in order that they might
pray for neighbors who have yet to start their journey with Jesus.
Let's see how it all got started.

Shawn and Carla Caldwell's Neighborhood

We began our neighborhood ministry by praying for all the neighbors we knew by name. My son Kyle and I (and sometimes Carla, my wife) would walk our street, praying as we went along. We would pray down one side of the street, turn around, and then pray over the other side. After a month or two, we reached out to a few of our neighbors who we knew to be Christians and asked if they would be interested in meeting at our house to pray for the neighborhood. The response was very enthusiastic.

At our first gathering, we enjoyed a very simple meal (hamburgers and hot dogs), followed by a discussion that covered a wide gamut of prayer needs for our neighborhood. Everyone prayed after the meal, and we decided that we should try to do this on a monthly basis.

"MANY ARE OF DIFFERENT BACKGROUNDS WITH ONLY TWO COUPLES ATTENDING THE SAME CHURCH."

Over the course of the first year, we ran into some difficulty finding a mutually agreed-upon time to meet, and at times the monthly meeting stretched out to every five or six weeks. That became too irregular, so now we gather every third Sunday. Many who attend regularly come from different backgrounds, and only two couples attend the same church.

I can say without hesitation that it has been both a blessing and a blast getting to know our neighbors. We all really look forward to getting together and praying for each other, and for the neighborhood. I do think the meal and fellowship has greatly contributed to the appeal and consistency of our gatherings.

Because we are all from different backgrounds and churches, we don't agree on everything, but we are definitely united in our belief that praying for our neighborhood is a good thing, and that getting to know our neighbors is the icing on the cake.

After a little more than a year of praying together, we decided to invite our unchurched neighbors to one of our monthly meetings. As one would imagine, we didn't observe our regular prayer time together. Even giving thanks for the meal was a bit out of the ordinary for some guests. Yet God is growing us together into a very close group.

The fact is, I didn't even know most of these people before I started down this path, but now I look forward to seeing them each month. We all enjoy a true sense of neighborhood and community…and this in a group of people whose paths might never have crossed.

We continue to pray, waiting expectantly for the Lord to move. After all, this isn't just about making friends; it's about leading people toward the kingdom of God.

A time for reflection

Shawn and Carla's story is just one way that Christians are coming together in neighborhoods today. I have found that what the Lord initiates with Christians varies in different neighborhoods. As you read this and the other stories, hopefully your idea of what neighboring looks like is expanding and you are opening up to possibilities you hadn't previously considered. The Lord is extremely creative and will lead you in what He has in mind for your neighbors. You may choose to begin to pray like Shawn, Carla, and Kyle did. Remember, it is not about trying to make something happen, but about praying, waiting, watching, and joining your Father when He opens doors for you in your own neighborhood.

Respond

Do you have a regular time of prayer for your neighborhood? Sit down and go over your weekly schedule. Carve out at least ten minutes to pray for your neighbors every week. Of course, you can choose more than ten minutes a week, but it needs to be a time period that you can actually follow through with.

_____

_____

_____

_____

_____

Shawn and Carla Caldwell have been married for thirty-five years and have six children and seven grandchildren. They have lived in Acton, California, a rural area north of Los Angeles, for most of their married life. Shawn is a general contractor, and Carla is a homemaker who enjoys time with her grandchildren and her livestock. Both are active with their church as well as with the Gideons.

29

Neighbors from Two Different Churches

A new command I [Jesus] give you: Love one another. As I have loved you, so you must love one another. By this everyone will know that you are my disciples, if you love one another. —John 13:34–35

As we begin to love our actual neighbors, we will probably encounter people from other congregations who just happen to live in our neighborhoods. Are we going to avoid them or are we going to invite them to join us in loving our neighbors as ourselves? If we are obedient, we will submit to Jesus' new commandment to "love one another."

Philip Yancey pointed this out in his book *Vanishing Grace*: "When I ask, 'Tell me the first word that comes to your mind when I say *Christian*,' not one time has someone suggested the word love. Yet without question that is the proper biblical answer. 'As I have loved you, so you must love one another,' Jesus commanded His disciples at the Last Supper. He said the world will know we are Christians—and, moreover, will know who He is—when His followers are united in love."[12]

There is no better place for the world to see this kind of love lived out than in the very neighborhoods where we Christians live. Jim and Doris and Cal and Alice had the opportunity to experience this kind of love as neighbors. Both couples attend different churches but experienced the beauty of loving one another. Consequently, their neighbors have been the beneficiaries of this kind of love. Observe how the relationship of these two couples grew through the years and what the Lord is now doing through them with their neighbors.

Jim and Doris Lloyd's Neighborhood

We've lived next door to Cal and Alice for over thirty-three years. Over the years, as we've transitioned from one life stage to another, so has our relationship with Cal and Alice. As I consider each stage or chapter, I can see how God was preparing us for His purpose and His will in our neighborhood. The journey has been an eventful one with lots of laughs as well as some tears.

When we first met Cal and Alice, we were in our mid-thirties with four small children, ages six, four, two, and eight months. Cal and Alice were on the downside of their careers and looking forward to retirement. Our relationship could be characterized as "Greetings, Feedings, and the Secret Passage." In the early years, we casually greeted them and demonstrated friendship toward them. They were friendly and hired our kids to feed their pets when they were traveling or away from home. It was also a cooperative relationship. Since our boys' basketball hoop was next to the fence, inevitably the ball would bounce, get thrown, or be tipped over the fence separating our yards. As young boys will do, they'd hop the fence and retrieve the ball. Cal noticed this and placed a ladder on his side of the fence to make it easier for the boys to get back to our yard. This led to discussions, and we installed a secret passage between our yards. Soon a hinged twelve-inch fence board connected our yards and made ball retrieval much easier.

The secret passage served as a good metaphor for our relationship, still separated by a fence, but open to possibilities, and we caught glimpses of each other and how we lived as neighbors over the years.

This causal relationship continued for the next several years, and frankly our lives were full and overflowing with work, family, church, and all of the kids' activities. During this season my wife, Doris, and I were challenged to live out our faith where we lived. Consequently, we expanded our life group and invited Cal and Alice to join us in the Bill Hybels' series *Just Walk Across the Room*. They accepted the invitation.

This study very naturally gave us a window into the lives, hopes, and dreams of our neighbors. It deepened our relationship and provided us with an opportunity to speak truth into their lives and for them to speak into our lives as well. We got to know their children, who all lived out of town, and connected with them as we lived apart from our parents as well. We also began taking time to look for ways to encourage and support Cal and Alice.

Shortly after this we transitioned from Greeting and Outreach to the third stage in our journey: Intentional Neighboring.

Scripture is very clear that we serve a missional God and He sent Jesus to us. Jesus reminded us of this in John 20:21, when He sent us out into our neighborhoods as well. Our children have since left home and married, and have homes and children of their own. We still live next door to Cal and Alice, but now our ministry has moved from the casual and convenient to intentional. I didn't know what this meant, and I certainly was not prepared for what God would do in my life, the life of my family, or the lives of Cal and Alice. Lynn Cory pointed out in his book, *Neighborhood Initiative and the Love of God* that neighboring is easy, but not simple. It's inconvenient and it's messy, but when you've done what God is calling you to do, there is also great joy, hope, and blessing.

"I NEVER IMAGINED THAT THIS WOULD BE WHAT GOD WAS CALLING US TO."

So, when Cal and Alice asked for help with their spa, I became their "pool boy." Later, I recruited my son-in-law, and we built a pool cover. Then Cal's health began to deteriorate, and Alice had back surgery. So we provided meals, drove them to doctor's appointments, and ultimately visited them and prayed with them during their hospital stays. Alice slowly recovered and returned home. Unfortunately Cal continued to decline. After several hospital stays, he was transitioned from home to a temporary care facility and then to permanent care.

Driving home from visiting Cal one day, Alice was stopped at a light. Her car was rear-ended and pushed into the car ahead of her. Just like that her car was transformed into an accordion, was rendered un-drivable, and she was stranded. A young man pushed the car to a nearby gas station. That's when I got the call. I arrived to find Alice shaken, but otherwise unhurt. While waiting for the tow truck we went to a small café and had a bite to eat. We talked through the accident, and I provided assurances and confirmed that we would walk with Alice through the process. You could see the anxiety and fear lift from her shoulders… she was not alone.

Around this time, Alice shared with us how much Cal enjoyed listening to the old traditional hymns. So I downloaded several albums on an old iPhone and got him headphones. Then he could listen to those hymns right from his bed without disturbing his neighbor. When we visited, Cal sometimes would be in his wheelchair and we would explore the care facilities. We talked together and chatted with nurses, other patients, guests, and pretty much anyone walking the halls or sitting in the recreation room. We took him to lunch in the cafeteria, and Alice would try to get him to eat. Cal was pretty picky about what he liked, and, seriously, I was never hungry when I saw what he was eating. You have to understand, Cal loved to cook and barbecue, he was adventurous in the kitchen, and the healthy diet being prescribed was not something he enjoyed. Sometimes we'd bring him grapes…he ate those!

On January 23, a Tuesday, we went to visit Cal, since he was not doing well. The family, Alice and the kids, decided to move him to hospice care. We arrived at the hospice facility following Cal's transfer at about 5:30 p.m. His blood pressure was low so Alice decided to spend the night. We left at around 6:00 p.m., returned home, and picked up some things for Alice. Doris fixed her a sandwich. We had Life Group at our house that evening, but after praying and sharing, we cut it short.

By 9:00 p.m. we arrived back at the hospice facility where we stood around the bed comforting Alice and listening to hymns softly playing in the background. I had the opportunity to hold Cal's hand and read the Twenty-Third Psalm when he slipped into eternity. I never imagined that this would be what God was calling us to do when we began our journey into intentional neighboring. Not only was God using us to comfort Alice, but God Himself was comforting us as well. You see, after Jesus told His disciples that He was sending them out in John 20:21, He gave them the Holy Spirit as the Comforter and Helper on their missional journey as sent ones (John 20:22). He sends and we go. As we go, He provides the resources that we need for our journey.

Cal's passing moved us into a new relational dynamic with Alice. Both Doris and I have lost our parents over the past several years. We were also "distant children" to our parents just as Alice's children were "distant" to her. As we considered this new normal for Alice, we recognized the unique position and opportunity God had given to us. We could be Alice's "nearby family." What a blessing for us. Doris would provide a few meals during the week and call her regularly, and I took on the responsibility to take out the trash, change the occasional light bulb, and do other helpful things around the house.

Alice is a regular at our holiday meals and special events. She is part of our Life Group and helps us with various neighborhood ministries. We take pictures of these times and send them to her kids. Our kids and grandkids all recognize Alice as one of the family. On one occasion, our three-year-old grandson was scrolling through pictures on my wife's phone when he came across one particular picture and loudly exclaimed "Alice!" Yes, it's official when the grandkids recognize her and give her hugs as greetings... she is indeed part of the family.

A time for reflection

Cal has gone on to his heavenly home while Jim and Doris and Alice continue to carry on the earthly work down here in loving their neighbors. Soon after I received Jim's story, he sent me the following in a text: "By the way, Alice is coming over this afternoon to help Doris make enchiladas. We do dinner for neighbors on Tuesdays, mostly young families, both parents working with little kids. I'm calling it 'TN3' (Tuesday Night Neighbor Night)."

Wouldn't it be wonderful if Christian neighbors from all over the country began to team together in neighborhoods to love their neighbors like these two couples have? Do you know Christian neighbors in your neighborhood? If yes, what would it look like if you began to open your homes to one another and develop meaningful relationships with a vision to love your neighbors? May the Lord allow your adventure with your neighbors to be as fruitful as that of Jim and Doris's.

Respond

Why do you think Christians often don't partner with Christians from other congregations? What do you think Jesus would say to this kind of behavior?

_____

_____

_____

_____

After graduating from Humboldt State University, Jim Lloyd got a teaching position in Fresno, California. He met his wife, Doris, and they raised their family of four children, which has now grown to nineteen, including spouses and ten grandchildren. Jim has been an educator for over forty years. He was raised in a Christian home, but it was in college that the faith he grew up with became personal. Jim has continued in ministry both in his church, in his community, and in his neighborhood where he currently leads a neighboring-focused study. God sent Jesus, and Jesus sent us. Enjoy the journey.

30

The Miracle for Five Guys

Then the righteous will answer him, "Lord, when did we see you hungry and feed you, or thirsty and give you something to drink? When did we see you a stranger and invite you in, or needing clothes and clothe you? When did we see you sick or in prison and go to visit you?" The King will reply, "Truly I tell you, whatever you did for one of the least of these brothers and sisters of mine, you did for me." —Matthew 25:37–40

It is easy for us to dehumanize and categorize the people Jesus mentioned here. But He lifted these people to a higher level by indicating that when you care for one of them, you are caring for Him. Through the years, I have spent time talking with and listening to homeless people. It has helped me remove a critical view of them. I have discovered that homeless people are all uniquely different. Some intentionally have chosen to live on the street. Others have fallen on hard times and are trying to get their feet back on the ground. Some of these people do not want anything from you, while others appreciate any help you can give them.

I remember talking with a homeless man in Palm Springs, California. We sat down on a bench together, on the main street in town, and talked for quite some time. He shared his background with me. He used to be a tennis coach in the local high school. During our warm exchange, I was heartened by this man's life and grateful for the privilege to spend time with him. The homeless are our neighbors and are to be cared for, as Jesus pointed out to His followers. Our neighbors are not just those who live next door, but those who cross our path, as John points out in his story with Dave.

John Tolle and Four Guys' Neighborhood

Five Guys is the name of a fast food restaurant chain, but we were five men who intentionally stepped out and stumbled our way into neighboring a homeless man.

Unkempt and unshaven with matted hair and rotted and missing teeth—you get the picture. This was Dave five years ago, and today he is my friend and brother in Christ.

Most nights we saw Dave asleep in his encampment adjacent to a local freeway. And every morning he made his way to a local restaurant to buy a cup of coffee with the money he had collected while panhandling the day before. He pretty much kept to himself, though he'd engage if talked to. One Sunday, I was introduced to Dave by a group I came to affectionately call, Panera Church. They graciously extended themselves to this wonderful man and allowed me into their fledgling circle of friendship. That was five years ago.

"HE CREDITS GOD'S 'LOUD VOICE.'"

Nationally ranked as a high school swimmer, Dave earned a full-ride scholarship to a prestigious, sports powerhouse university. He was on top of the world. But! Injuries, drugs, partying, and a whole host of other human demons robbed him of his privileged life, and time reduced Dave to the loneliness of homelessness. It didn't happen overnight, but it happened. Make no mistake, Dave was bright, gifted, and personable, yet he'd fallen on hard times, and much of it by his own choosing.

All the negative characteristics that defined this homeless man acted as barriers that kept people like "us" away from him, and God had His hands full dealing with us. In time, each of us came to understand that we needed Dave as much or more than he needed us. He was our neighbor. Jesus said so (Luke 10:25–37).

The process of neighboring has been a rewardingly costly one, as love and obedience usually are. Time, energy, finances, you name it. It was a slow process. Then we lost him. He disappeared. Years of investment down the tubes, or so we thought.

About a month later we received a message. Dave was in the hospital barely able to communicate. He'd had an aortic aneurysm. He credits God's "loud voice" as having prompted him to dial 911. Barely conscious when the paramedics arrived, Dave died while being rushed to the hospital. Marginally revived by the ambulance crew, he was rushed into emergency surgery only to suffer a heart attack and stroke while on the operating table.

Recuperation was difficult, but his recovery was miraculous! God has restored Dave's health. Today he has a full-time job at the very restaurant where we met. He rents a room in a home and attends church regularly. He belongs to a men's Bible study group and has lunch with his pastor every week.

God gave each of us to the other as neighbors.

The willingness and obedience of five men continues to be a neighborly blessing to Dave, and his loving friendship to us has enriched us beyond description. Dave is a miracle…and a miracle to five guys.

A time for reflection

John's story helps to humanize and remove the stigma that we often place on homeless people. It is a wonderful account of redemption. What John doesn't go into detail about is how long and difficult this process was. What God called John and his four friends to do may not be what He calls you to do. Caring for a homeless neighbor is best seen as an opportunity (*kairos*) where God lays an individual on your heart in the moment, or over time, and directs you to care for that person in some way. I caution you, as Jesus did His own disciples, to be "as shrewd as snakes and as innocent as doves" (Matthew 10:16). We can be moved by John's story and foolishly walk into a situation where we have not heard from God and find ourselves in a situation we may regret.

Respond

Helping a homeless neighbor should include prayerfully considering the following: (1) Have you asked the Lord if it's your role to help in some way? (2) What would the Lord like you to do to help this person? (3) As John and his friends exemplify, is this something you can do with other people? (4) What kind of commitment is reasonable for you to make to this person? (Remember to seek counsel from wise people.) (5) Is this person receptive to or agitated by your attempts? In other words, is the *kairos* moment now? (6) Chances are the person has a lot of need, but your job is to listen for God's leading, not to rescue the person from what you can see with your eyes. (7) Educate yourself on services provided for the homeless within your community and consider connecting a homeless neighbor to services and free resources that already exist in the community.

_____

_____

_____

_____

_____

John Tolle was born in Los Angeles and grew up as a missionary kid in Central America and a pastor's kid in California. While attending college he answered the call of God to prepare for pastoral ministry. He has served in a variety of ministry roles but is best known for being a pastor. John and his wife, Rosemary, reside in Thousand Oaks, California. They have four grown and married children and ten grandchildren. It doesn't get any better than that!

31

When Neighboring Challenges Come from Within

> You have heard that it was said, "You shall love your neighbor and hate your enemy." But I say to you, Love your enemies and pray for those who persecute you, so that you may be sons of your Father who is in heaven. For he makes his sun rise on the evil and on the good, and sends rain on the just and on the unjust.
> —Matthew 5:43–45, ESV

Maybe you have heard the saying "The church is the only organization in the world that shoots her own wounded." This is not a new phenomenon. We see it clearly manifested when the apostle Paul was in prison and critical believers on the outside were trying to stir up trouble about him (Philippians 1:15–18). Maybe you have experienced this yourself or you have observed others in the body of Christ going through difficult times and believers were disparaging of them. Now take this into the neighborhood. Neighboring is difficult when there are conflicts or challenges with those who do not yet embrace Christ. It can be even more trying when the challenges or conflicts come from those within the body of Christ. Have a firsthand look at what Tom and Cami experienced in their neighborhood.

Tom and Cami Anthony's Neighborhood

What started as a grand desire to reach a neighborhood together turned into the most difficult season of our lives. A new neighborhood was being built west of our city, and a family in our church asked us to consider purchasing homes together. The dream was to build in proximity in order to partner in neighboring and reach the families around us. After much prayer, we decided to move.

A third family joined the process, and the first six months in the new community brought exciting opportunities and dozens of new relationships. We found families moving into a new community were eager to get to know their new neighbors. Block parties, soup nights, and regular times connecting in the street in front of our homes ensued. Neighborhood Bible studies started, and people who had never experienced Christian community were drawn to what God was doing. The Lord was definitely moving in the hearts of those around us.

About that time, our family was experiencing a significant transformation. We had six children under the age of twelve and were about to adopt two more, a niece and nephew, out of the foster care system. While we were not idealistic regarding how disruptive this transition would be, there was no way to know how much of a challenge this would create in our family life.

Imagine two children pulled from their home by Child Protective Services and placed into foster care for *five years*—yes, *five years*—coming to live in another state with a pastor's family and six children they hardly knew. Needless to say, it was not a smooth transition in those early months. While God was definitely shaping the hearts and lives of all ten people under our roof, we were a messy work in progress. Support groups for us, counseling for all, and therapy for the adopted kids proved very helpful. A variety of people provided support, and God was in the center of our mess. In exasperation one day, I confessed to a trusted Christian mentor, "These kids make me so angry!" His response penetrated my heart when he said, "They don't make you angry. They simply reveal what was already there." During this season, what we felt we needed most was our Christian neighbors' faithful support. What actually happened was the exact opposite.

"AT ANY MOMENT, WE FELT COMPLETELY BETRAYED AND ABANDONED."

In our desire for authentic community we shared the struggles, the emotions, and the sinful attitudes being brought to the surface in our lives. Instead of extending prayer, encouragement, and love, we received accusations, withdrawal, and even threats. It was one of the most difficult times in both of our lives. At that moment, we felt completely betrayed and abandoned.

What we didn't know was our situation had touched a wounded place deep in the heart of one of our Christian neighbors and also had brought other childhood traumas to the surface for a few others. While we had started a grand adventure to "reach the neighborhood," God had other plans for transformation right within our group. While we became broken relationally with the Christians on the block, God was still working, bringing neighbors to faith and involvement in the church. And He was doing His work of transformation in the hearts of the Christ-followers on our street by not allowing pain, trauma, childhood experiences, and unseen wounds to go unchecked.

If the story ended there, it might be difficult for us to want to jump into loving our neighbors and our Christian brothers and sisters. We might be reluctant to love neighbors if our efforts only resulted in pain and sorrow. But our God is a redemptive God. A few years after God had called us to a different state and another church, we received a letter in the mail. It was a letter of apology. Over several pages, one of our neighbors poured out her heart of conviction and repentance, and her desire for relational reconciliation. God performed a miraculous work of healing in many of the hearts involved. What started as a grand desire to reach people around us who did not know Jesus Christ turned into a redemptive story of forgiveness, healing, transformation, and reconciliation.

A time for reflection

It is very hard to read what Tom and Cami went through, but their story imparts a very important perspective. Neighboring can be portrayed as an idyllic adventure, especially for believers working together in a neighborhood. Tom has given a realistic picture that we all need to hear when it comes to loving our neighbors. Neighboring is not a blissful endeavor that is wrapped up with a pretty bow on top. Though the Great Commandment is not a spiritual discipline— in fact, it is the aim of the spiritual disciplines— nothing brings about personal transformation like obedience to loving God and loving our neighbor.

Have you already begun to love your neighbors and become disillusioned by a negative encounter with a neighbor? Have you said to yourself, because of this discouraging experience, "I am not doing that again"? Is it time to reevaluate that decision and talk with a respected friend about what you went through with the hope of taking baby steps back into loving your neighbors? Remember our God is a redemptive God who works in the mysteries of the unknown. What He invites you into may look different than your plans but will always be for your highest good. Like Tom's friend revealed, this experience could be an opportunity to uncover the things in our hearts that need healing. If you are new to neighboring, are you willing to step into it even though you might encounter difficulty with a neighbor? Take time to consider these things before stepping out.

Respond

How does Tom and Cami's story help you continue to be encouraged when neighboring isn't smooth sailing for you?

Tom and Cami Anthony have been involved in neighboring for over twenty years and have served in a variety of roles on church staffs in Indiana, Texas, and Colorado. They currently live in Colorado Springs and are involved in "transforming lives from the neighborhoods to the nations" at Mountain Springs Church. Tom serves as the executive pastor of ministries and outreach. They have eight grown children and are expecting their first grandchild in 2019.

32

Surprised by Kindness

But the fruit of the Spirit is love, joy, peace, forbearance, kindness, goodness, faithfulness, gentleness and self-control. Against such things there is no law. —Galatians 5:22–23

Acts of kindness touch hearts deeply. Once when I was washing car windshields in front of a fast-food restaurant, I asked a woman if it would be okay if I washed her windshield. I assured her I would do it for free and that there were no strings attached. She was visibly surprised by the request, but she apprehensively accepted. As I was washing away, I sensed someone inside the restaurant was staring at me. I turned around to see the woman who had accepted my offer watching me in amazement. She motioned for me to come inside. When I went in she said, "No one in this world would do what you are doing!" Much to my surprise, I responded, "I know, but I am not of this world." This is the beauty of God's Spirit coursing through our lives…you get involved in doing things that are otherworldly that touch people's lives profoundly. Note what happened in Neftali and Deborah's neighborhood when a group of believers worked together to show the kindness of God to their neighbors.

Neftali and Deborah Santiago's Neighborhood

One day a team from our church joined Neftali and Deborah Santiago in their neighborhood to take on some extensive projects. The team trimmed two large mulberry trees that were hanging over a new neighbor's home, hauled away large discarded items, washed cars, and built a fence. The neighbors were greatly impacted. The man whose trees were trimmed said that he couldn't afford to have them trimmed because all his savings had gone into buying a home in this neighborhood. He went on to say, "They never treated me this way where I used to live." He and his wife were incredibly grateful. Later, his wife told me that she'd shared the story at her job in a family-run business and everyone was surprised by this act of kindness.

"WHAT YOU ARE DOING IS WORKING...DON'T STOP."

One of my favorite stories from the Santiagos' neighborhood came the Sunday following one of our workdays there. An elderly woman named Joanne showed up at one of our church services just after the service started and sat next to me (Lynn) in the front row. She asked if she could tell everyone about her experience with what we were doing in the Santiagos' neighborhood. At first I was somewhat reticent, not knowing what to expect, but I threw caution to the wind and introduced Joanne as the Santiagos' neighbor.

She seemed very comfortable in front of everyone; her comments were moving and humorous. Joanne told the church how meaningful our visits to her home had been to her. She had experienced a family tragedy the year before and had been processing the grief with a counselor. Around the time we showed up at her door, the counselor had encouraged her to go to church. "What you are doing is working," Joanne said. "Don't stop."

Joanne's words that morning encouraged all of us incredibly. The Lord was pleased because the neighbors were experiencing His love through us. Doors were being opened for the gospel through genuine love and concern for people.

A time for reflection

Joanne's timely word came more than ten years ago because she experienced the Lord's kindness through His people. The apostle Paul pointed out in Romans 2:4 that the kindness of the Lord leads to repentance. The people in this story were surprised by the unconditional love of believers, and they were moved by our no-strings-attached acts of kindness. Have you considered putting together a team to help some needy person on your street?

Respond

Is the Spirit encouraging you to do some otherworldly act of kindness with someone in your neighborhood? Who might that be, and what is the Lord asking you to do?

_____

_____

_____

_____

33

A City Set on a Hill

You are the light of the world. A town built on a hill cannot be hidden. Neither do people light a lamp and put it under a bowl. Instead they put it on its stand, and it gives light to everyone in the house. In the same way, let your light shine before others, that they may see your good deeds and glorify your Father in heaven.
—Matthew 5:14–16

A pastor friend of mine once said to me, "The hardest thing I have ever done in ministry is to lead my congregation to love and care for their actual neighbors." It is so countercultural for the Church because churches in our culture are not designed to do this. However, obedience to Jesus requires us to let our light shine in the context where He has placed us and to let His light emanate from our homes into the surrounding darkness. As our light begins to shine in our neighborhoods, it has the potential to change whole cities. Observe how the Lord's light is working its way out from Bob and Sandy's neighborhood to the city of Fullerton, California.

Bob and Sandy Jensen's Neighborhood

My wife, Sandy, and I moved to Fullerton, California, in 1979. When we arrived on our shady, quiet street, we learned that we had been adopted into an active, connected community of neighbors. Since the early 1950s, that tradition of connectedness had influenced the character and quality of life on the street. At the center of all those activities were Barbara and Bill Kent, who served as the leaders of our neighborhood.

The Kents helped organize monthly teas for the women, where the activities of the street were discussed and planned, allowing for full participation from all of their neighbors. The Kents helped put on Halloween and Christmas parties as well as a Fourth of July block party each year. That all-day event included a breakfast buffet and tennis tournament, a themed parade with neighbors living on an adjacent street, children's games, swimming, a potluck dinner, and fireworks in the cul-de-sac at the end of the street. Before each Christmas party Mrs. Kent presented a slide show of Fourth of July party photos from the year before, five years before, ten years before, and so on. She took great pride in enlisting her audience's participation in identifying all of the children in the photos, and she shared stories about the children and their families. In many cases those children, now grown up, were returning to the street to bring their own children to the Richman Knoll July Fourth party.

Mrs. Kent also published a street map with neighbors' first names and phone numbers. Beyond that, she offered our family access to her swimming pool, which is where our children learned how to swim. If anyone was seen driving at unsafe speeds on our quiet street, it was Barbara who knocked on that family's door and asked them to drive more carefully. When people moved away, it was the Kents and other neighbors on the street who organized send-off parties. Years later when Sandy and I read the *The Art of Neighboring* by Jay Pathak and David Runyon, we realized that the Kents had practiced the art of neighboring for decades.

Many changes have occurred in the years since the early 1950s, but the vision of the Kents and their early neighbors has continued. After Bill died and Barbara moved into an assisted living facility, Sandy and I, eager to be involved in the lives of those living around us, felt drawn to continue many of the neighborhood activities the Kents began. We help organize the Fourth of July events, host Christmas open houses, pumpkin carving parties, and ice cream socials. And we share these responsibilities with a closely connected network of volunteer neighbors. When new folks move to our streets, we welcome them into a culture of connectedness that has lasted nearly seventy years.

"WE BELIEVE WE CAN CHANGE MINDS ABOUT WHAT IT MEANS TO BE A CHRISTIAN."

During this time of neighborhood involvement Sandy and I became involved in global and local missions through our church. We have asked the Lord for opportunities to honor Him through service to others, and the Lord has abundantly answered that prayer. We've met some remarkably inspiring kingdom workers through the years. Among those people have been Jay Williams, our local outreach pastor who now runs OC United (a nonprofit organization seeking to make a difference in our city), authors like David Runyon and Lynn Cory, activists like Matt Svajda of Fiducia (a neighboring ministry initiative), and other incarnational missionaries whose faith calls them into action in highly imaginative and compassionate ways.

Sandy and I have tried to combine what we learned from the Kents and other people committed to living intentionally in their communities with what we've discovered by reading books on the topic, participating in Bible studies, attending conferences, and going to workshops focused on neighboring. With the help of Matt Svajda, we also launched neighboring classes at our church. Two of the most important lessons we learned is that our love for our neighbors must be offered without strings attached and that we need to consistently pray for our neighbors and for opportunities to demonstrate the gospel in action.

Neighboring and local outreach service came together in the spring of 2019, when our city service day, Love Fullerton, assigned a large team to tackle weed abatement on an acre of tall weeds and underbrush for a family struggling with health issues and related financial problems. Because that family has struggled since coming to the street, Sandy and I have decided that we are called to love them and pray for them, expecting nothing in return. As we work with city officials, vector control, and the fire department about conditions on their property, we continually remind ourselves of Jesus' call to "love our neighbors as ourselves."

We are all works in progress, and our outreach to our neighbors will continue to evolve. The people on our street know that we are Christians, and it is important to us that we reflect those values in our relationships with them. By making ourselves available to our neighbors and deepening our relationships with them, we believe we can change minds about what it means to be a Christian.

A time for reflection

Bob and Sandy's lives were deeply influenced by the Kents. Had they not lived in Barbara and Bill's neighborhood, the trajectory of their lives more than likely would have taken a different course. The lives of those who live in our neighborhood are very precious to God, and we have the opportunity to touch their lives in a transforming way. They undoubtedly influence ours in return. How are you being changed by the people in your neighborhood, and what kind of influence are you having on them?

Respond

What are some regular events that bring out your neighbors throughout the year? What can you do in your neighborhood to gather and get to know your neighbors during these events?

Bob and Sandy Jensen attend the First Evangelical Free Church of Fullerton in Fullerton, California, where they serve as missions coordinators for their adult fellowship class. They have served on the mission board and have participated *in or led six short-term global missions teams. Bob serves as a leader for Love Fullerton, and Sandy serves on the board of Bless Vietnam Initiative. Sandy is the communications director for the Far East Broadcasting Company, an international broadcast ministry. Bob is retired from Fullerton College, where he served as a theatre professor and dean of fine arts during a span of thirty-five years. They have three children and two grandchildren who live in Southern California.*

34

Making Apprentices of Jesus

> Then Jesus came to them and said, "All authority in heaven and on earth has been given to me. Therefore go and make disciples of all nations, baptizing them in the name of the Father and of the Son and of the Holy Spirit, and teaching them to obey everything I have commanded you. And surely I am with you always, to the very end of the age." —Matthew 28:18–20

In Jesus exists all power and authority. Before He ascended into heaven, Jesus, much like a sheriff, deputized His disciples to assume His responsibility and act on His authority. What responsibility was He passing on to them? They were to extend the invitation into apprenticeship with Jesus. Even as He was returning to heaven, Jesus said to them, "And surely I am with you always, to the very end of the age" (Matthew 28:20). His Spirit would join them, and us, in this work of making disciples.

Jesus instructed His disciples that they were to baptize His new apprentices into the triune God and teach them to be obedient to everything He commanded. This invitation to make disciples wasn't for a select few in the Church but for all. Thanks to the obedience of Jesus' followers, the gospel spread rapidly throughout the known world for three centuries. But when the Church, the confessed followers of Christ, was limited to the work only the leaders did, the progress of spreading the gospel was impeded and the Church itself weakened. A lack of obedience to the Lord's instruction in the Great Commission by His followers today is one of the greatest omissions of the Church. We have lived vicariously through our leaders rather than being personally obedient to the Lord's command.

My story is more of a confession than anything else, but it has opened my eyes to how significant it is to make disciples of Jesus right in my own neighborhood and to have this understanding of how God desires to move His kingdom forward right where we live.

Lynn and jo Cory's Neighborhood

Jo and I have been loving our neighbors since the 70s and have served in three different neighborhoods. Through the years, we have initiated countless activities in those neighborhoods. Our home has always been open to our neighbors, and we have seen God work in some amazing ways. However, from time to time God has asked me to do some things that were threatening, or at least I thought they were at the time. I have experienced how He has taken me slowly, step by step, to the next thing that He has asked me to do with my neighbors. Each time, I dragged my heels until I gave in to His direction and stepped out.

The Lord has made it clear to me that loving my neighbors is more than just doing nice things for them. The Great Commission, making disciples, plays an essential part in neighboring. The Lord put it on my heart to start a neighborhood Bible study. Fearful, I put off doing what He asked me to do. I thought, *What would neighbors think if I promoted a Bible study in our neighborhood?* I supposed they might distance themselves from me if I did.

I continued to grapple with it until one day I received a text from a neighbor that said something like this: "If you ever start a Bible study, would you invite me?" I knew the Lord was speaking to me through this neighbor, and I thought, *How should I go about it?* Finally, I could put it off no longer, so I designed a flyer for our neighbors, and this was the basic content of the invitation:

Neighborhood Discovery Bible Study

Lynn and jo Cory's Home

This is the first time we have ever done anything like this for our neighbors, so we would love it if you could join us. We already have some neighbors who have accepted our invitation. This group is not associated with any church… it's just for neighbors who desire to learn about what God says in the Bible. Each of us will have an opportunity to give our input and learn together. We are very excited to invite you. If you would like to bring a dessert item, please do. Oh yes, bring a Bible if you have one or we can supply one.

It's going to be fun!

Much to my surprise, the Lord began to open the door to different neighbors who wanted to join us. Some I invited personally, some responded to the flyer, and one flagged me down as I was walking through my neighborhood. She pulled me aside and said, "May I talk with you about something? It's spiritual." We had never talked about anything spiritual prior to that. We talked at length in front of her house, and after our discussion I invited her to our Neighborhood Discovery Bible Study that meets on Monday nights in our home. She asked, "You have a Bible study on Monday nights right across the street?" And I responded with,

"Yes, and we would love it if you would join us." My fears were dispelled, and through the Bible study God has connected us as neighbors in a very special way. These neighbors have become our close friends, and not just geographically. We have a genuine concern for one another; we share meals together, and we help each other. The wonderful thing about a neighborhood Bible study is that everyone is just a short walk away. We are experiencing community much like the early Church.

"LOVING MY NEIGHBORS IS MORE THAN JUST DOING NICE THINGS FOR THEM."

One of my favorite memories is when one of our neighbors in the Bible study stopped me on one of my walks and asked if I did counseling. I said yes. She responded with, "How much do you charge?" I said, "Nothing." We arranged to get together on a Saturday morning when Jo could join us. Our neighbor shared with us, and I pointed out to her that the Lord could take care of her situation if He were in her life. She expressed interest in that possibility. So, I shared with her the story of how I came to the Lord and how I prayed with a friend and invited the Lord into my life. She said, "I would like someone to do that with me." I asked her, "Would you like to do that right now?" And she said yes. She gave her life to the Lord and was baptized in our pool with those in our Bible study sharing in her celebration. She has commented on different occasions how much the Bible study means to her. She has gone through the books of John, Philippians, and Acts, and is presently going through the book of 1 Peter with us.

Another member of the Bible study group reflected on her experience with us this way:

> I was eager to deepen my journey toward Christ by studying the Bible in a more organized, structured way. The ideal opportunity came with an invitation from jo and Lynn, who not only had solid academic knowledge of Scripture, but an abiding and deeply personal love for the Lord. I had seen, firsthand and over many years, how they applied His Word to their lives and to every relationship.
>
> When we began our study nearly two years ago, I knew I would grow in my knowledge and understanding of the Bible—and I have. What I did not expect was how our time together with our neighbors (some of whom I knew casually and some I'd only met at the Corys' neighborhood gatherings) would turn us not just toward the Lord, but toward each other. Each week, we bring our Bibles and our open hearts, and we continue to learn about the Lord and each other. We share private struggles and triumphs, we tease and laugh and encourage one another, and we pray together. I've been deeply affected.
>
> When my teen daughter was in a terrible accident last year, I texted Lynn almost immediately. I found enormous comfort in our group during the first few traumatic weeks and in the months of her subsequent recovery as I was enveloped in love and concern, and lifted by prayer. I'm grateful, too, for whatever encouragement or connection I'm able to offer the others. I've come to admire and love their goodness, intellectual rigor, and devotion to the

Lord. And I so enjoy the sheer variety of personalities and points of view!

Recently, I have even found the confidence to speak more readily to others about the Lord and the many rewards of my quest to know Him more fully, and that's another unexpected and wonderful outcome of our Bible study. I continue to look forward to Monday nights at the Cory dining room table as one of my favorite weekly commitments!

Now, as a new little community of believers in our neighborhood, we plan events together and share in the opportunity to hand out event flyers and work together on BBQs, host potlucks, welcome new neighbors, and plan other neighborhood gatherings. You can watch our neighbors' responses to a breakfast that our group put on in our backyard.

Go to www.youtube.com/watch?v=5_QYKI5yxic
or search YouTube.com for Lynn Cory,
and you'll find my channel.

I have been involved in small-group gatherings with believers since the '70s, but this experience with those in our neighborhood has given us a greater sense of community because of our geographic proximity to them.

A time for reflection

Though it took me way too long to initiate our neighborhood Bible study, another mistake can be made in starting a neighborhood group...starting too soon. Some people have jumped right into starting a Bible study with their neighbors and have found that there has been no response or, even worse, that they have alienated themselves from their neighbors. If you have ever thought about starting a Bible study with your neighbors, here are a few things to consider before stepping out:

1. Have you been praying about starting a Bible study and developing meaningful relationships with your neighbors?

2. Has the Lord been prompting you about starting a Bible study?

3. If you are starting the group as a couple, how can it become a team effort?

4. Are there other believers in your neighborhood who might like to join you?

5. Begin to ask the Lord to show you how He would like you to go about promoting the study. Flyers may be helpful, but give them a personal touch by talking with your neighbors about the Bible study when you hand it out to them.

6. When you start a Bible study with your neighbors, design it so that everyone participates. This engages each person, leaving you free to be the host, and God is free to lead the course of your time together.

7. Here is the format I used for our Neighborhood Discovery Bible Study to ensure everyone could participate.

   Discovery Bible Study*
   - Start with a short prayer.
   - Ask, "What are you thankful for?"

- Ask, "What is stressing or challenging you?"
- Ask, "Is there anything we can do to help relieve the stress?" (ex. prayer, help in some way, etc.)
- Bible Study

  1. Ask everyone to read a portion of the chapter in the Bible. (If someone is uncomfortable reading, let that person know he or she doesn't have to read.)

  2. Walk through the text asking some of the following questions:
     - What does this Scripture reveal about God?
     - What does this Scripture reveal about humanity?
     - What does this Scripture reveal about the life God has for us?
     - What other questions or insights do you have about this Scripture?

  3. How can we apply these discoveries this week?

  4. Is there anyone who could benefit from what you have learned or want to apply?
     - Close with prayer. (If you sense that others are ready to pray, ask them if they would like to pray.)
     - You will find that as you get to know one another better, your exchange will flow more freely.

8. How much of a time commitment are you able or willing to give to a study, as it will likely evolve into deeper relationships with your neighbors?

Conclusion

For the Spirit God gave us does not make us timid, but gives us power, love and self-discipline. —2 Timothy 1:7

It's Your Turn

I hope the Lord has inspired you through these neighborhood stories and you have gained some insight as to how to more effectively love your own neighbors. To help you get started in your own neighborhood, I am providing a helpful tool titled "Prayer, Care, Share." Keep in mind this is only a tool.

"THE BEST SUGGESTIONS WILL COME FROM THE HELPER."

You will need to move out in your own neighborhood in the way the Spirit of God leads you. The NI website (neighborhoodinitiative.org) and *Neighborhood Initiative and the Love of God* (available at the NI website) both provide a wealth of suggestions and guidance for connecting with your neighbors, but these are only limited resources. The best suggestions will come from the Helper, the Holy Spirit, as you submit to His lead and ask for insight as to how best to reach your neighbors with the love of the Father.

Prayer, Care, Share

Prayer

Devote yourselves to prayer, being watchful and thankful.
—Colossians 4:2

Prayer for our cities begins at home and in our neighborhoods. Here's a simple plan for prayer walking your neighborhood.

- **Pray** for your neighbors by name, considering their physical and spiritual needs, concerns, and health. Ask the Lord to show you what He is doing in your neighborhood. Instead of praying for a specific outcome to the situations you see, consider proclaiming the truth that God is greater than the need. For example, if I pray that little Johnny's cold will be cured today, I am dictating what God must do, but if I thank God for being bigger than this situation, I am allowing Him to have His way. Maybe Johnny's discomfort causes him to be still, which he's been needing for a while. The point is, we don't know what to pray, but the Spirit will intercede for us (Romans 8:26). While you are walking and praying, engage any neighbors you may meet along the way.

- **Wait** on God. Your Father is already at work in your neighborhood. Wait for Him to invite you into what He is doing. This is a specific kind of waiting—waiting with great anticipation. In this phase there is no action taken, but rather it allows the opportunity to practice patience and stillness. Imagine it like a conversation where you have shared (prayed) and are now waiting for the other person to respond. There may be uncomfortable silences. When discomfort comes from a yearning to see God move in a tangible way, this is a great opportunity to surrender any specific expectations to Him.

- **Watch** to see what the Father is doing. As you are praying, He may reveal things through something He puts on your heart or speaks to you, as you talk to a neighbor, or as you see a need. This often looks like an opportunity that presents itself or a random idea that pops in your head.

- **Join** your Father as He invites you into what He is doing in your neighborhood. Respond! Take the initiative. Enjoy the *kairos* adventure!

Care

When he saw the crowds, he had compassion on them, because they were harassed and helpless, like sheep without a shepherd. —Matthew 9:36

Care flows from a heart that is filled with compassion for those in your home and neighborhood. If you love them as yourself, your heart will go out to the people in your neighborhood. As you pray for them, you will begin to care for them the way you care for yourself.

Here's where you start:

- **Co-labor with God:** Once the Lord invites you into what He is doing, recognize that the work is His doing and that He will give you the grace to care for those in your neighborhood. Feeling inadequate to the task is normal as God desires to shepherd you along the way He's prepared.

- **Initiate Conversation:** The needs of neighbors are manifold. All you need to do is take some time to talk with your neighbors, and before long they will fill you in on the needs of others who live on your block. Invite neighbors over for dinner or coffee and they will open up like a flower about what is going on in their hearts and families, and about the matters that concern them most.

- **Listen:** Learn to ask good questions and then "listen." Did I say listen? Resist trying to interject things to say while they are talking. It shuts down the flow of things coming from their hearts. Offer to pray for them if it seems appropriate.

- **Meet the Need:** When a neighbor's need becomes apparent, meet the need. Our neighbors will never listen to our words until they know we really care. Meeting the need may be just listening, helping with something around their home, or providing food for them. The Lord will not prompt you to engage in a codependent relationship where you become the savior. Jesus does the saving, but He may hand you a life preserver to toss out to someone. Caring for others opens their hearts to relationship. Don't be surprised if they want to help you in return. On the other hand, don't be shocked if they never offer to help you.

- **You Can't Do Everything:** Keep in mind that every need in your neighborhood is not your responsibility. Sometimes you will have to say no. A neighbor may want to take advantage of your kind heart, and that's where you need to be as wise as a serpent and as innocent as a dove. For some, this may be hard, but you want to be about your Father's business, and remember part of the Lord's command was to love your neighbor "as yourself." Self-care is essential to being available to care for others. Serve from the abundance in your life, always being mindful to let the Lord fill you up first.

- **You May Need a Partner:** Enlist others in your neighborhood to help you with larger tasks. Look for caring neighbors who would like to help you bear the burden of a particularly needy neighbor. Don't do it alone. You will burn out and give up on caring for your neighbors.

Share

And pray for us, too, that God may open a door for our
message, so that we may proclaim the mystery of Christ.
—Colossians 4:3

If you look at the accounts of Jesus sharing about Himself and the
gospel of the kingdom, you will never see Him do it the same way
twice. No, never. Sometimes an account happened with very few
words, like those spoken to the man next to Him on the cross,
but on other occasions they were lengthier. I love observing how
Jesus beautifully revealed who He was to the woman at the well.
He was a master of the moment (a master of *kairos*) for sharing the
gospel. The Lord will give you these kinds of moments with your
neighbors. It may be in a one-on-one situation, over a meal, in a
small group setting, or…you name it.

Be Ready to Give an Answer

When God opens a door for the gospel, allow the Holy Spirit
to speak through you as you share your story and then His story. We see the apostle Paul using this approach in the book of
Acts. Become effective in sharing the gospel in this manner with
your neighbors. Role-playing is a very helpful tool for training, so
practice with a trusted, godly friend. Remember your goal in the
process of relating to your neighbors. The goal is not to clinch the
deal with a sinner's prayer; God may have someone else assigned
to that task. The goal is relationship.

Share Your Story

Write out your story and include these three parts:

1. What your life was like before you met Jesus.

2. How you came into a relationship with Him.

3. What your life is like now that you have Him in your life.

Be able to share your story in just a few minutes, depending on the situation. Generalities are not engaging, so access the power in your story by relating a specific incident in which you knew God was real for you.

Share His Story

1. Read the Gospels so you become familiar with the big picture of Jesus' life, His ministry, the cross, and the resurrection.

2. Memorize verses that you can share when you are imparting the gospel. The more verses you memorize, the freer you are when sharing the gospel.

3. Of course, you can take your neighbors to one of the Gospels and let them read it (or you can read it). Ask them to share their impressions as they read. So often, we want to give our understanding first, but allow them to respond with their thoughts. When they begin to ask you questions, then you have earned the right to speak (1 Peter 3:15).

Listen to Their Response

Ask your neighbors what they think about what they have heard or read to see if they are receptive and open to the Lord. It is completely acceptable to not have all the answers for them. They can and will have to flesh out many of their own questions with the Lord directly and through other resources over time. However, you can always point them in the right direction.

If Your Neighbors Are Responsive, Stay with Them

If someone listens to you and to what has been said, stay with that person, as Jesus said. You have found a person of peace. Devote time to the relationship and help that person in a new walk with the Lord. Help grow that new believer's understanding of the Scriptures. Start with one of the Gospels. You may need to create space in your life as the need to be present with this person unfolds.

Also, the person of peace, more than likely, has a network of relationships in his or her neighborhood, family, and friends. We see this over and over in the book of Acts where whole families and extended family members came to faith. Think multiplication. From the beginning of creation, the Lord emphasized to Adam and Eve to be fruitful and multiply. The same is true with the advancement of His kingdom. You needn't fear this because the Lord goes before you and will never leave you (Deuteronomy 31:8). He walks beside you whispering *this is the way, walk in it; walk in* kairos (Isaiah 30:21).

Enjoy *The Kairos Adventure* as you join the Father in your neighborhood and beyond. May the Lord give you stories that will inspire others to love their neighbors as well. I would love to hear your story. Email it to me at lynncory@neighborhoodinitiative.org.

Notes

1. Center for Philosophy for Children, University of Washington, *Summary of "The Garden" in Frog and Toad Together* by Arnold Lobel (HarperCollins; First Edition October 3, 1979), philosophyforchildren. org, accessed September 19, 2019, https://www.philosophyforchildren.org/ questionslibrary/frog-and-toad-together-the-garden/.

2. Lynn Cory, *Neighborhood Initiative and the Love of God* (Colorado Springs: NavPress, 2013), 20.

3. Rick Rusaw and Brian Mavis, *The Neighboring Church: Getting Better at What Jesus Said Matters Most* (Nashville: Thomas Nelson, 2016), 80-82.

4. "Gilbert K. Chesterton Christian Quotes and Sayings," Allchristianquotes. com, accessed September 19, 2019, https://www.allchristianquotes.org/ authors/224/Gilbert_K_Chesterton/.

5. Michael Green, *Evangelism in the Early Church* (Grand Rapids, MI: Eerdmans, 1970), 210.

6. William Shakespeare, *Romeo and Juliet* (England: 1595) II, ii, 1-2.

7. Barna Report: Cities 2017 by Barna Group (Fresno-Visalia, CA City Report 2017–2018 with comparative data from the Pacific region), 25.

8. Brookings Report, https://www.brookings.edu/research/u-s-concentrated-poverty-in-the-wake-of-the-great-recession/, accessed September 19, 2019.

9. Used by permission, a paraphrase from a sermon given by N. T. Wright at Central Presbyterian Church, New York City, January 29, 2017..

10. David Sanford, *Loving Your Neighbor: Surprise! It's Not What You Think* (CreateSpace Independent Publishing Platform, 2017), 207-209.

11. Alan Doswald, *Pray and Do the Next Thing...* (CreateSpace, 2018), 132, 133.

12. Philip Yancey, *Vanishing Grace* (Grand Rapids, MI: Zondervan, 2014), 35.

Join a revolution!

What if Jesus' disciples actually demonstrated obedience to His commands that we love our neighbors and one another? Imagine the whole church in every community in our cities working together to bring the love of God to every neighborhood. What if each of our homes became centers for the loving ministry of Jesus? What if every one of our neighbors then began to experience the extravagant love of God? People would say, "I want to have the kind of love they have! And Jesus would be pleased."

Through the love and power of the Holy Spirit, we can and will see this in our day. Neighborhood Initiative is for those who want to join a Jesus revolution of love in our cities, neighborhoods, families, workplaces, and schools.

Join the movement!

Imagine pastors and leaders in every city working together to bring the love of Christ and His kingdom to every neighborhood. What if pastors embraced Jesus' Whole Church and genuinely demonstrated love and concern for one another? What if followers of Jesus in every community worked together to model Jesus' love and bring His kingdom to their neighborhoods? This is what the Spirit of God is initiating in our day. *The Incarnational Church* is for those who want to join this movement, so we will see revival and awakening in our cities.